THE MAN FROM
THE SUNRISE SIDE

THE MAN FROM THE SUNRISE SIDE

Ambrose Mungala Chalarimeri

Magabala Books

The Man from the Sunrise Side
Published by
Magabala Books Aboriginal Corporation
PO Box 668
Broome Western Australia 6725

Magabala Books receives financial assistance from the State Government
of Western Australia through the Department for the Arts; the Aboriginal
and Torres Strait Islander Commission; and the Aboriginal and Torres Strait
Islander Arts Board of the Australia Council, the Federal Government's
arts funding and advisory body.

Thanks to the Benedictine Community of New Norcia Inc. for use of photographs held
in their collection.

Cover design by Narelle Jones/Jane Lodge
Cover photograph *Oomarri Rock Painting* by Traudl Tan
Designer Jane Lodge
Printed by Shannon Books, Victoria
Typeset in Stempel Schneidler 10.5/14

National Library of Australia
Cataloguing-in-Publication data

Chalarimeri, Ambrose Mungala, 1940–
The man from the sunrise side

ISBN 1 875641 02 5

1. Chalarimeri, Ambrose Mungala, 1940-. 2. Drysdale River
Mission–History. 3. Catholic Church–Missions–Western
Australia–Kimberley–History. 4. Aborigines, Australian–Western
Australia–Kimberley–Biography. 5. Aborigines, Australian–Western
Australia–Kimberley–History.
I. Title.

306.089915092

contents

the early years

observations of a Kwini man

continued...

Kwini tales of the dreamtime

animal yarns

working man

contemporary times

acknowledgements

My great thanks go to Traudl Tan, my partner, for helping me get the stories together, for her encouragement, understanding and patience, and for her thousand questions that never stopped, but pulled the stories out of me properly.

I also appreciate the assistance of the Australia Council for the Arts, which provided financial assistance to get us started on the project and Ansett Australia for donating a flight to Perth to check my family history in the State Archives.

My thanks must also go to my late brother-in-law and my sister Magdalene Maraltadj and their family, who invited us to stay at Warlngga (McGowan Island Beach) near Kalumburu. Also thanks to some very special people in Kalumburu: Aunty Mary Pandilo, old Manuela Puruan, Aunty Dolores Cheinmorra and her children, Liduvina Undulghumen, Eileen Fredericks, Ruth and Lesley French and their family, old Hector Dangal, William Punjak, our special friend and helper George, Sister Lex and Sister Monica at the clinic, and the mission staff. Thank you all for your kindness and your friendship!

I thank the Emergency Services for rescuing Traudl and me in 1998 from a bushfire in a very remote location, when our vehicle broke down on the way to Oomarri; for the wonderful hospitality of the staff on Troughton Island in the Timor Sea where we were taken to; and for organising the return to our vehicle. Thank you also to Justin, the Manager and his men, who worked near Oomarri at the Beta Creek Striker Resources mining camp the same year, for treating me, the traditional owner, with respect and courtesy. Thank you also to Luis Hissink who delivered our petrol drum from Kununurra to the bush – without you we wouldn't have been able to live on my country that year.

Some of the people of Kalumburu very kindly let us record some of their own stories, as originally we wanted to get them all published. Unfortunately because of a death in my family at the time, and the fact that no accommodation could be found in the settlement when we needed it a bit later, we regret we were unable to continue with these recordings.

about the style

My first language is *Gunin*, some people call it *Kwini* but really Kwini is my tribe. The meaning of that word is *the people from the sunrise side*.

With the old people I mostly speak in our lingo, but now English is used more and more by the young ones, and our language is slowly disappearing. Not many people left that can speak it. Some young people don't know it at all.

All my stories are told on the tape recorder then put on the computer and then Traudl and I make 'em good. Some things I say, Traudl types straight onto the computer. They're written down the way I talk, only bin straighten out a little bit. That's the way I talk to people when they're not used to Aboriginal way of talking.

Sometime we use words everyone knows, but when we use 'em, they might have the meaning different. Like when I say *in a tree*, that really means *under a tree*. When I want to say something is *in a tree*, I'll say *on top of the tree*. A *quiet snake* means a *harmless snake*. The word quiet can also mean tame or domesticated, like what we call a *quiet horse* when it's been broken in.

I might one time say *I went* and at another time I say *I bin go*; the meaning is the same. Many times our people use the time words for what bin happen before or now or next time in different ways, but people will know from the story line what is right. If the words are used a bit different, it's because that's the way we talk in our English, they're not mistakes. I think people will understand anyway.

Ambrose Chalarimeri

about the process

Ambrose and I met in Port Hedland in 1994. He was studying a course in horticulture and I was there on a work contract as executive officer to the Director at Pundulmurra College. Ambrose told me in 1995 he had wanted to write his stories for a long time but couldn't find anyone to help him, so I offered. We wanted to record his and some of his people's stories on tape, then transcribe them for a book. Ambrose said he wanted to write his stories for his people and for others who know little about Kimberley Aboriginal history.

We thought it would be good if we could include members of his family in the project, and other people from Kalumburu as well.

I bought a second hand ancient model Toyota Landcruiser, so we could tackle the bush tracks in the Kimberley. We visited the Kalumburu community and obtained approval for the project. Then I went begging and wrote twenty-five funding applications to see if we could get some help. Finally we received a small grant from only one funding agency – Australia Council for the Arts. Gratefully we put new tyres on the vehicle, had some maintenance and repair done, bought the recording equipment, put our belongings in storage, organised a trailer and moved to Kalumburu. We had been assured that we would get accommodation in Kalumburu, but when we arrived, the house was derelict and could not be fixed. We lived in a shack on a beach at a lovely place called Wulngga, or McGowan Island Beach, looking after tourists who came to camp there in the dry season, at a place which belonged to Ambrose's brother-in-law.

That year there was a very sad death in Ambrose's family and our plans for recording their stories had to be postponed indefinitely. The recordings we made of other people in Kalumburu also had to be put on hold because, after one year, we ran out of accommodation as well as money. We returned to the Pilbara where I finished a prior work contract.

During the next twelve months, Ambrose and I concentrated on his stories only, but managed to record and work on just one story a month because of my full time job. When I finished my work contract, we lived in the bush on Ambrose's country Oomarri for some weeks. Then we moved to Perth to complete Ambrose's stories before I returned to paid work.

Some of the work for this book was not exactly easy for me. I have come a very long way from the other side of the planet into the Aboriginal world. By the time I met Ambrose, I had worked with Aboriginal people and was glad and proud to have friends among them. I thought I had a bit of an understanding, but nothing had prepared me for Kalumburu and people like Ambrose.

Ambrose and his people have most generously and willingly opened a door to a Kimberley Aboriginal world that sometimes made me delirious with the joy of being alive and able to share it, and on other occasions, I sat down and cried in utter sadness and frustration. I consider myself immensely privileged to have gained a deep insight into what it is like being an Indigenous person in our time and place, and within the structure of a society, where materialism far outweighs the value we place on people, which is in total contrast to traditional Aboriginal values.

Before we set out to live in Kalumburu, we were anxious to start the recordings because of the age and frailty of the few precious old people still alive then in Kalumburu. We were right in our fear as several have since passed away, each of them taking with them a personal treasure of local and tribal history and experience that will never be known.

Each time we managed to record some stories, I felt very humble and privileged to be able to share the information, and what a treat some of the recordings were!

'Unungule unungule minya ...' (once upon a time...) that's how old Aunty Mary Pandilo started her stories with her voice rising and falling in anticipation of what she was going to tell me. She taught me some Gunin language. This is how I described my recording experiences at the National Oral History Conference in Alice Springs in 1997:

> Many times I have been mesmerised by the magic produced by the story-telling technique itself, irrespective of the content. One very old lady obviously enters another world when she tells her stories. Perched on some rickety plastic chair under

the shade of a tin shack with the wooden support structure on the point of collapse from white ants, a far away, distant expression spreads over her wrinkled face and her voice assumes dimensions not present in her ordinary speech. There are traces of spirituality and mysticism, a deep respect and love of the land and its people. The voice is rich in intonation, emphasis and nuances, and the rise and fall within a sentence or passage creates a captivating melody of its own. It is such an immense pleasure to listen to the old people when, with their words and body language, they conjure up aspects of the world of their past, a world so very different from our own. I felt like being taken by the hand and led across a cultural divide which would be impossible to cross unassisted.

1997

I wish more non-Aboriginal people could have similar encounters. Through my experiences in Ambrose's Aboriginal world, my life has been immeasurably enriched and I am so glad I could help him share his experiences and stories with readers everywhere.

Traudl Tan

On Monday 17th of July, 1944 more Kwinis arrived, amongst them Tjalarimeri, nursing a baby girl and a boy of five. Having lost one of his two wives, who was the mother of the children, he did not know how to feed the baby girl. She had been able to survive by sucking and pressing the breasts of some compassionate old women. As we have often seen, these women who are past the age of child-bearing, produce some milk when continually sucked by children.

Tjalarimeri has another wife, a younger sister of the deceased, who never had a baby, and despite the persistent suckling of the little girl, she produced very little milk, so that the little girl was more than a skeleton. We have called her Magdalene and the doctor thinks she is about 8 months old.

Her brother Mungala, who is about 6 years old, is more wild than can be imagined. The father seldom came to the mission with the family.

Kalumburu War Diary
Fr Eugene Perez O.S.B.

Gunin and other words

boodjelooma . . . . . . sea cucumber
clapsticks . . . . musical sticks that beat time
cumbungi . . . . noxious weed
cunmunggoo . . . . . bush bread
didjeridoo . . . . woodwind musical instrument
djadja . . . . daddy
doonggool . . . . tassles
kartiya . . . . white people
jilinga . . . . bush woman (maybe spirit)
joolooroo . . . . name of a dance and song
joonba . . . . a type of dance of the Kwini people
jorrmulla . . . . name of a Kulari peoples' dance
jimi . . . . good spirits
junggao . . . . / . . lizard
kooro . . . . cypress pine
koyo . . . . crocodile
Kul . . . . name of a mountain
kurranganda . . . . . name of dance and special boards used for dance
Lalai . . . . Kwini Dreamtime
lirrga . . . . type of dance
meniwurra . . . . flying fox
moodooroo . . . . hairstyle for dance
murr . . . . riverine tree with big leaves used for canoe-making
ngadarri . . . . hats made from paperbark
ngoonooroo . . . . . . string
ngurraworri . . . . . . bush apples
nyogoo . . . . hip covers
Oonggoorr . . . . Rainbow Serpent of the Dreamtime
pardao . . . . bandicoot
pulga . . . . name of a dance and song
pulmurra . . . . wooden boards used in dance
punurr . . . . bush turkey
ulan . . . . large tree with small leaves, rough bark, thick trunk
umba . . . . kangaroo
wala . . . . whip snake
wanda . . . . bowl
winjibut . . . . Ironwood tree (eucalypt)
woorro . . . . a lean-to shelter
wulngga . . . . 2m bush yielding edible tuber; name of a place
wungga . . . . song and type of dance
yaourr . . . . water goanna
yirumi . . . . name of a dance

Orthographic note: Spellings of Gunin words in this book are rendered from speech. The Gunin language of the Kwini people is the subject of a proposed publication titled *Kwini Winya Baara Bilangayi: These Words are from Kwini People,* by the Kimberley Language Resource Centre.

the early years

Where I come from

I am Ambrose Chalarimeri and I am from the Kimberley. My mother was called *Tandoalo*. She passed away after my sister Magdalene was born. My father was *Piurungei (Piuri) Chalarimeri (Tjalarimeri)*. My bushname is *Mungala* and my totem is the *janggao*, a lizard about a foot long.

The name Mungala is the word for the throat of that lizard. My brothers had names that come from other body parts of the lizard, like my brother, Martin. Well, his traditional name is *Muddenmoro*, that is the word for the belly part of the janggao. We brothers all have the same totem.

The lizard stays in trees much of the time. Smaller ones you find in houses too. They are very handy because they eat cockroach and white ants, you know, in the timber and they catch flies. They live in the roof or a tree.

My family belong to a place called *Oomarri*. That's the name of my country. It's called King George River lately, but Oomarri is the traditional name of that waterhole. There is a spring there and that's where I was born. The lizard swam across the little spring, went to that small island in the middle of the creek. This is my Dreamtime story. I was told that by my old people that have all passed away now. I'm nearly the only one left now that was born in the bush in those days. The old people told me stories how I was born at that river there. My tribal country is the area between Kalumburu and Oombulgurri; that used to be called Forrest River Mission.

My father had several brothers—each had one or two wives and each family group live separate, but not too far away. The families used to get together sometime for corroborees, dances, or to bury their dead. Or they traded ochre for large shells that they used to carry water, or sugarbag, that's honey, or ground flour from seeds. Sometime my father used to leave everybody and go for tribal meetings. He went alone, just took his spears, that's all. He used to camp halfway, make fire so 'nother people know he's coming. He tell 'nother tribal groups to get together for meetings, do things together. They had like peace talks sometime, so there wasn't any fighting. My father was good at this, that's how all the people know him well.

Now I want to tell you something about the bush food we lived on, things like bush potato and yams. People had to dig for *cunmunggoo*, that's bush bread. Then we had bush apple and wild tomatoes, bush almonds and plums, they all grew at the beginning of the Wet and get ready to eat round Christmas time. To get them can be hard work. You must know where to look and when it's wet it's not easy to get to places, even on a foot. You have to find plenty and open them. The palm shoots are good. You can eat it raw or cooked in the ashes. It tastes like cabbage, you eat the young shoots and the inside part. Bush honey we call *wana*. People used to climb up to get it in the trees. The bees don't sting and they're very small.

We also hunted emu; go very early, well before first light when the emus make a sound like a drum beat. It's easy to sneak up on them at that time when they just stand around scratching themselves, still in the dark. We also had *punurr* (bush turkey), which is a bit hard to catch unless you have a hunting boomerang that is good and heavy, you can knock a person down with that. People also eat kangaroo, dugong, turtle, lots of fish and oysters.

When they hunt for kangaroo people used to go with the spear before. They used to go and get ant pad from termite mounds, break it up and rub it in the armpits so the kangaroo won't smell you with the wind. Ordinary anthills they break up, or mud will do, too. Ant pads have a special smell like the ground when it's wet. First of all people sneak closer and closer without a sound.

Sometimes they light a fire round in a circle, leave a gap where the 'roos can come out and then spear it as they rush out. The kangaroos can't see through the smoke. After people take the guts out, empty all the pipes, put it back then, sew it up again. Sometime they put hot stones inside, then bury it and cook it in the ashes— big one take longer to cook. You leave it in the skin 'cause the skin help cook it.

All my people from the coastal side in the north are tall. The language we speak is the *Gunin*, some also call it the *Kwini* lingo, that's what we talk. That lingo has nearly died out now. The young people speak mostly English these days. Some understand Gunin, but don't speak it—people have to live in another world now.

Old man Yogin

The old man Eugene was a member of my family. He is my father's brother, but I still call him my father. We don't call him uncle because, in the Aboriginal way, this is not right. We children always call our father's brothers: Father, and our mother's sisters are still also our mothers.

My father's brother, Eugene, was younger than my father. My father was the oldest and tallest of all the four brothers, and now I am the tallest in the family. The people on the mission called him Eugene, but the Aboriginal people called him *Yogin*. He was not called Chalarimeri; he's got 'nother name. So has my brother Martin's father; that old man was called *Maolul*. He carry me too when I was small. He was working in Truscott*, he was big like Martin, but my father was tall and high and thin. I look like the people on the rock paintings in my country, people from saltwater look like that, all tall. My country is the river country but we hunt near the seaside too—I was born at the fresh water.

We went to visit Forrest River Mission—me and Yogin and others. It was a three-day walk from Kalumburu to Forrest River Mission. Sometimes people took longer. Yogin took me from Kwini camp in Kalumburu, and set out a bit further away along the Laoar Creek, where we collected paperbark upstream. Some other people came too: Victor Martin, and my grandfather and grandmother. They carried me sometime. I don't know how old they were but they were fit to carry me then. Other family members came too, about half of the family went. My father was in the group. Don't remember if my mother was with us really. Don't remember when I saw my mother last.

We had no other children on the walk to Forrest River then, because no other children were born in my family after my sister, Magdalene. My brother, Roland, in Oombi was born later in 1960s. My sister, May, and him have same mother but different father, one of my father's brothers.

I know all my father's brothers but they passed away when I was in the mission. Don't know where or when they died. We could find no record in Perth about them. Martin's father is the only one buried in the Kalumburu cemetery. While they were working unloading the barge at Longani Landing, he suffered a heart attack and died. At Forrest River Mission, my people camped in the outside camp, so they weren't recorded in the books, no record of them at all. Only sister May's father is mentioned in the archive. His name was *Mung-gula*.

Don't know Yogin's totem. I saw him again when I came home to Kalumburu from Argyle Station where I was working. In Kalumburu, I went to the Kwini camp and they all cried for me because they were happy to see me again. They heard I was working on the station. That was about 1963. I left Kalumburu 1962. My family hadn't seen me for one year, even Christmas time I was on the station.

The Kwini camp was still going strong then, but it finished in 1970 or 1980. In 1963 I spent two months in Kalumburu, but stayed at the camp in the daytime now and then, and sleep at my sister Magdalene's house. The Kwini camp now is only a paddock fenced in by the mission but not used for anything. Only one old hut is still standing now.

We just sit down in the camp and the people tell you stories of what happened. Sometime people in the camp went on holiday; they go to Pago, or Forrest River Mission. During the dry season they go to King George River, that's halfway to Forrest River. Kalumburu Mission ring up superintendent to say people are coming. People got rations from the mission for the trip: tea, flour, tobacco, that's why they told the mission when they were going. Also because some of them worked in the mission, and they need to let mission know when they going, they asked Father they wanted to go on holiday. Don't know how much rations they got, people would divide it up and carry it, good enough for everybody. Sometime they hunt along the way for kangaroo and goanna.

They would start walking early in the morning before the sun came up. When it's up then they will be far away. If it's hot they stop under a tree near water and then they start in the afternoon and walk again when it is cooler. Sometime, when it is full moon, they walk all night if they feel like it. They spread out when they walk, not one behind the other.

Everybody knows the way. They knew the distance; they walked it up and down all the time. Sometime the path disappears but they know the landscape. From Kalumburu they follow the road to Mama Waterfall, then to Ngalaworri Waterfall, then along the road to Barton Plain, Jiliowei, across where there used to be a house. Somebody knocked off the tank from that house. There was a homestead there. From Barton Plain just go along the river and follow the jump-up, that's the main passage. Barton Plain is a little bit this way, the other way is past Carson River and behind, there is a passage in the hill and you follow that. That's where Dennis Howard shot *punurr*, bush turkey, that's the road, leaving Carson River that way. People follow that path before the white people came. Then that track became the road later, and that track went all the way down to Forrest River Mission.

From King George River, you go to Berkeley, then from there, to Forrest River. You are just about there. The mining company made roads later.

I came back from Forrest River Mission when the war was finished. I was in the dormitory then—later on, not straight away, I think. People went to Forrest River Mission because they had family there in the outside camp. The camp was where there are houses now. The boab trees were there but small, the camp was at the back, near the swamp.

I saw my father last around the age of ten. My father left for Forrest River Mission again with other people and left me behind in the dormitory. From there, I don't know what happened to him. After I was in the dormitory for a long time, I forgot about my father after all. He must have bin died in the bush and no one told me about that. Much later somebody told me he died somewhere near Forrest River.

Yogin stayed behind then in the Kwini camp in Kalumburu and he was still around while I was in dormitory. I called him *djadja*—daddy.

He told me about the land, how I was born there at that waterhole at Oomarri, at King George River. I told him, 'I never heard about that.' He said, 'You was small, swimming in the water-hole.' Yes, I was born there, that's true from his own word. He told me I was sleeping in the water, and then he came to look. He found a little child. He looked and found a little boy; that was me. He told me himself, in the dream he found me. That was true. That is a Dreamtime story. He dreamed about how he found me and then he took me from that waterhole.

When I left the mission and came back for holidays, I used to go and visit him, told him about work on the station and how I came to Wyndham. He never went to any town; he only went to Forrest River. He worked along the fence line along the Drysdale River with Laurie Waina, Francis Waina and my brother-in-law. He didn't go anywhere, he wouldn't know what a town is, he only stayed in the bush. I come to Kalumburu on an aeroplane then. He used to tell me when somebody passed away, or about Kulari people. He used to tell me more about Dreamtime stories and about ghost or devil.

Yogin liked me. He looked after me all the time. He looked after me more than my own father. Father Rosendo, who lived on the mission, told me too, 'Might be this is your father,' he told me that. Maybe it was my father. Might be he only take care of me, I am from his oldest brother. Father Rosendo said, 'Eugene care more for you than the other man' (meaning my proper father). Yogin had no children, he only collect me, that's all. He had two wives but they had no children, I don't know why.

Once, when Martin and I were grown men, we all went to Anjo, Truscott, to work for the mission and Yogin came on the barge too. The Australian Defence Force had built a military base on Truscott Peninsula just across the bay from Kalumburu. We were sleeping on the beach near a fire. One night we run out of tin tobacco and Martin woke me up and said, 'Go and ask daddy for smoke.' Yogin was sleeping a distance away and I walk across and woke him, 'Hey, daddy, got any smoke?' He gave me handful from his tin under his pillow and said, 'That's for you and your brother.'

Yogin was still there when I left Kalumburu to work on the station and he was there 'til 1968 when I returned for holidays—that's when I saw him last. I worked in Derby then.

After that, he went away; don't know when. Twenty or thirty years is long time, not easy to remember. 'Yogin went away to the bush,' people said, 'he's gone.'

Yogin was a happy man. He used to dance *joonba* and make up songs. We found one of his songs on tape in Canberra in the archive. He used to bring corroboree from Forrest River when all the people were still alive, the older ones. Somebody said he had a long beard, but I don't remember. I don't know the Aboriginal name for Forrest River, the missionaries named it that.

I reckon he was the one who was making that smoke when you and I* went there to Oomarri (King George River) in 1996, just before the wet season. As we walked, following the riverbed toward the north, suddenly, smoke was rising up just ahead of us like somebody was walking and lighting fires one by one. It was very near. Sun was just this way ahead of us. We follow the water because that always flows north. The smoke was straight ahead, then fire was coming on the side. Yogin could have seen us from long way. Maybe he did know we were there. He could climb up some lookout and (had) seen us, perhaps. Lot of mining people say they saw a man's tracks all the time. I would've been very happy if he came out in front of me. I could've told him who I am and talk to him. He could show me where he lives or if he needs anything.

Straightaway I knew that it was the old man Yogin who lit the fires. I know that there were no other people in the area at the time because the Wet was coming. Everybody knows that the old man Yogin lives at Oomarri. At the same time, I could see a storm coming in the distance. It was very hot and it was hard walking because we had to climb over rocks and up and down the riverbed. That's why I didn't think of going to see who lit the fires.

* *Ambrose addresses Traudl from time to time.*

Yogin lived in the bush because he had 'nother woman. First wife he had he married in the church in Kalumburu Mission. Her name was Dorothy and then he left her when he was a pensioner. He had 'nother woman called *Mooneroo*. He ran away with her. In the old days, men used to do that when they left one wife and took another one. They would go away in the bush. Men were not allowed to stay in the mission with two wives. Mooneroo belong to *Walmbi* tribe from around Mount Elizabeth Station and Gibb River area. Her proper husband was *Jun-goo*. He was in the leprosarium in Derby. Later he died in there. Mooneroo lived with Yogin at Oomarri in the bush. After a long time, she left Yogin and walked back to Kalumburu by herself through the bush, more than a hundred kilometres. There was no road then, she just walked through the bush. The mission sent her back on the plane to Mount Elizabeth Station, because she wanted to go back to her people and she died there.

My brother Martin knows the story. I think he saw Yogin once there at Oomarri. Food was left out high on a table at one time and it disappeared. Martin was there and he saw footprints. He talked about seeing him, but that was a long time ago. Aunty Mary Pandilo told us about him, too. Perhaps the old man is frightened of going back. Nobody knows. I couldn't find the reason for it. Maybe he doesn't like to show up once he left. Maybe he preferred the tribal way and he thought he wouldn't return, just go away, maybe he didn't like to leave his country. Bush life was easier, no one to bother him there. He didn't like to stay in the mission because they didn't let him have two wives like before in the old days. Bush life was good.

Nobody don't know if the old man is still alive.

Mission life

I am going to talk about life on the mission when the war (World War II) was ended. All the nuns had been away at New Norcia, far away, and when the war was over they all came back to Kalumburu on the state ship *Koolinda* with Father Boniface. He then became the superior in the mission. He lived in the mission before the war when Father Thomas was in charge. People knew Father Boniface and liked him.

Mary Pandilo was the first Kwini baby born in the old Pago Mission before they moved it to Kalumburu. Pago Mission was also called Drysdale River Mission before, and they move it to Kalumburu in 1937, because they ran out of water at Pago. Mary was big then and the only person who looked after the children, when the nuns were away. Many of those people in Kalumburu now, they were children then, and I was the smallest at that time. We were all living at Tingun Paddock. It's a little way upstream from the mission. It was a lot of trees there and people moved there, because the mission had been attacked and bombed by the Japanese during the war. Several people were killed in that raid, Father Thomas, the superior and five Aboriginal children. One of the girls killed was Manuela Puruan's first daughter. She only had two children.

Nuns came back and everything was settled down. When they arrived, they were dressed up in a black habit of the St Benedict Order. Take a long time for me to know who they were. They all looked the same.

I didn't see white women before, only Brothers and Father Rosendo. I never saw the nuns before. They were in the mission before the war but I lived in the bush then. They all came on the army GMC truck from the barge at Longani Landing, on the old road right around the cemetery. We were all standing there waiting, greeting them and saying hello—I was frightened the first time when they came back to Kalumburu. I was new in the mission. We waited until they come and talk to us. Some gave us lollies. There were three Sisters, Matilda, Magdalene and Liduvina. Some of them are now in Spain. All were middle-aged or young, I couldn't tell, they all looked the same, we wouldn't know. We weren't interested to know about their age. They stayed in the mission for several years and when they left, others came.

The Brothers wore ordinary clothes when they worked, working clothes, shorts and trousers, but in church they wore black habits. Later on they changed to a white one—it was too hot to wear black habits. The Sisters' habits were black when they first arrived. We knew they were Sisters because the males wore ordinary clothes. The Sisters had parcels when they came, clothes and belongings. First they carried their luggage to the convent and then, from there, they start to look after us for a long time. The Sisters arrived in the afternoon. Next day we saw them and they worked. They speak English when they come and soon already pick up our language. They know mostly Spanish but learned language straight away. Oh, they also look after the fowls and they used to wash our clothes on Monday morning.

They brought us clothes from New Norcia. Every Monday we take our clothes and nuns wash it in big boiling copper that came with the barge. When I skinned a pig I used to boil the hot water in that same copper again. That same copper they used when they bottled tomatoes and, later on, they cleaned it and boiled all the bottles in the copper. It was round with a chimney on the side; it rested on a drum and the fire was underneath. It was quite big. It's still there today, near the washhouse at the back of the kitchen, bit over the left side. I am the one who helped Father Basil build the wash house, you know, where the old hospital is, the wash house was next to it. Later on Father Basil got the Aborigines to move the long concrete cement trough used for washing. It had a foundation and they chip it up, chip it up. The trough was about three metres long and very thick. They put crowbars and steel pipes across with a heavy rope and it needed lots of people to drag it to the new place. All washing was done by hand. Later they had three or four washing machines, but the trough is still there today. The Sisters also had irons, but different sort from today. It had opening for charcoal fire, special charcoal they put in to make it hot.

We children lived and slept in the dormitory. We didn't have bed sheets in the dormitory, only blankets and pillows. The nuns also used to cook for us. Brother Ildephonse—we only had one Brother then—used to grow vegetables. Later on the Sisters minded the girls and Brothers looked after us boys.

The beds were made of steel. We used to have mattress. Sometime we used to wash the blankets. It's hard work without a washing machine. We used to wash them in the river, the blanket that covered the mattress. 'Nother two or three we had to cover us when it's cold. Even the nuns and brothers didn't use sheets in those days. The mattress had some sort of brown wool in them, like coconut hair*. The dormitory was made of corrugated iron; the roof was timber and asbestos. It's still there today. There were two windows at one end, but there was no glass in them, only steel mesh, and the walls had ventilation shutters all 'round, no windows. There was one door with a lock on it that can be locked from outside only. We had one flour drum inside to make toilet in the night. It had no lid. In the morning when the door open, we use to go empty it outside in the pit. Some health people come one day and complain about it. When Father Sanz came back, he built proper toilet and shower block.

They had a toilet outside for us, round the back of the dormitory where the cashew nut tree is now. It was a big pit in those days. The seat was made of wood over a cut-off 44-gallon drum. The toilet drum sat on the boards. We had proper toilet paper. When the war was over, we were given heaps of paper left over from the defence forces stationed at Truscott, across the bay from Kalumburu. When we didn't have toilets that flushed, me and one brother used to go around and soak a hessian bag in diesel—then

Coir fibre

Brother used to light it and drop it in the toilet, once a month or every two weeks. Brother Ildephonse and me did that all the time. The diesel was mixed with oil in a Dingo flour drum. Brother used to say once we drop it, we leave it and let it burn. It was to take the smell away and act as disinfectant. Dettol was spread on the hard earth ground around the toilet. It was like a septic tank, the pit. Later we had a proper septic tank. It's all filled in now. In the dormitory we had two toilets and four showers. There was a covered archway built for us, we didn't have to go out in the rain.

On Saturday morning, all the boys used to clean the dormitory. Monday to Friday we went to school and Saturday we cleaned all the rubbish around the mission. We burnt it at the rubbish tip— we had that many tips, I don't remember which, I think it was near the airstrip side then.

Girls used to be in the dormitory near the nuns. The boys were separate. They thought we might sneak up to the girls. My brother Martin was in the dormitory too. When I was small I wet my bed sometime. Martin did too, and the others. When we wet the bed, they used to tell us not to do that. You had to walk outside and they hit us. I don't know why the children wet the bed. I think it could be because we were frightened. I was frightened at night sometimes. Yes, we used to live in a rough place.

Nuns, too, beat the kids with the belt or with the hand. They also use a whip. I saw it long time ago, the whip. You hold it there and it had six special strings like a kangaroo tail string, yellow colour and hard. It's about as long as my arm, had a handle out of rope and, at the end of the string, it had a hard dry thing, something like a sinew, like a fishing line. I think there was only one whip on the mission and it was kept in the monastery. Only the superior could hit the kids with it.

Only one Sister in charge carried the belt. They didn't carry it around all the time. They hit us in the bum. We never ran away, you can't do anything when you're small. We never thought of doing it, run away. We were in the middle of nowhere, nobody ran away. Martin went away, I think he didn't like it there, but that was later. Mostly people couldn't go anywhere.

When child was naughty at school they used to get belting by the Sister. I was the smallest one at that time and the girl one was Barbara Waina. Some of the people in our class are now dead. Barbara Waina, Lesley French and his brother Raymond were very small then; small children were never kept in the dormitory, they stay with their parents. When they grew older, they come to the dormitory. In the school we also had Martin, Robert Unangho, Ferdinand (I can't remember his 'nother name), from Gibb River, Lucy Unghangho, Rosary (Sylvester's mother) and Hilda Waina.

Sisters used to write on the blackboard and we had a slate each. Later we had copybooks, where you copy same as the other; then counting, we had exercise books for that. They used to give us addition tables, multiplying and what's the other one? Divisions. I forgot them all.

School used to start at eight and finish around three, I think. We enjoyed school because we children were all together. Middle of the week, we did drawing. Nuns were the teachers; they teach us how we must behave, how to be nice to others, how to speak to white people when visitors come, how to say "thank you" when they give us anything. When we used to ask for something we had to say "please". They said we must be good, to give example to the younger ones, not be late for school, not be late for church, be there right time and go to bed right time. We used to have small book where we can read easily and understand. They were in English, sent up from New Norcia and read: *This is the river, this is the land, this is a kangaroo…* That's how it was.

They also said we must not use bad words like swearing. If we did any bad things, Sister used to belt us with a cane on our hands. I think I finished school when Father Basil came to be the boss. He said to me 'Ah, you can go and work now.' And I did, I was around twelve then.

Everything was in Latin then

When I came to Kalumburu Mission as a child, I first went to Tingun Paddock because it was wartime and the mission was bombed already by the Japanese. Tingun was a place away from the mission buildings and safe from attack. You couldn't see it from an aeroplane; all you could see was trees. People stayed there 'til the war finished.

When I was baptised Father Rosendo said 'I put the name Ambrose for you in the book because Ambrose was a saint.' We were given a new name but we also keep our father's tribal name. Only I was baptised at the time—later on it was other people. Might be Brother Ildephonse was there and my father, nobody else from my family. Don't remember if my brothers were there. Somewhere I got a copy of the baptism recorded in the mission book. Father Pat sent it to me years later when I was working in Kununurra. I did ask him if he knows what date I was born, but there is no record 'cause I was born in the bush. Father Sanz said he thinks I was about six or seven years old when I come to the mission.

In the mission, children, when they're first born, got taken to the church for baptism. We altar boys just went to attend. Baby's real mother and father don't go. Mother was still in mission hospital then, only godmother go and hold the child, and godfather. Children were baptised soon as they're born, but not because they're sick. Children were born healthy but mission wanted to baptise them straight away.

Adults were also baptised sometime. They used to go inside the church door near where the holy water is all the time, that's where they're baptised. Or people got baptised in the camps. There were three or four camps near Laoar Creek then. I think old Peter's camp, Mary Pandilo father, lived there. People make camp in different places. Kulari people, they had pensioner camp the other side of the river on Kulari land. They lived in humpies; you could see 'em from the other side of the river. People from the mission used to go cross the river at Running Creek and bring food to the old pensioners, medicine, or baptise them. When the river flooded it was very hard to cross the fast-flowing water, so people used to start rowing across from upstream first and then you move across to the other side further down with the strong current.

When the river was in flood, they start on the boat from where the windmill is. Go upstream first with two or three paddles. They take rations, flour, tea and sugar for the pensioners. The men paddle all along the shore slowly, slowly, moving upstream and past where Laoar Creek flows into King Edward River. Normally in the dry weather, there are lots of trees along the river and it's hard to see clear up and down along the shores. In the Wet you can see clear along the river then because all the water is very high in flood, the trees are under water or just stick out.

We all used to stand and watch the dinghy move up carefully and see the boat turn round further upstream. One man is in the front with the paddle, the other two behind with the oars. They had to row stronger on the right hand side, so as to turn the boat more into the middle of the big brown river and toward the opposite side. We watch sometime with the rain falling down over the river and still see how the river bring the boat downstream, carried by the floodwater. Soon as they land on the other side we can see and shout, 'Oh, now they're safe!'

Once in two or three weeks rations were taken across like that. It was always Aboriginal men that did that, white people wouldn't know about the river. This day all right, they have outboard motor now, but controlling the small boats by hand is not easy when the river run so wild and fast.

We boys used to take some medicine to the camps, and we also went there for baptism sometime. When I got bigger, I was altar boy in the camps when people was baptised there. Father take service in the camps outside the mission and he used to take holy water to baptise people. Father used to baptise adults in the camp and give 'em new names. When we go to the camp, Father pick us up. We had to act like altar boys in the camp, only we didn't wear the church clothes. We use ordinary clothes; only in church we wear altar boy things, not outside. We walk to the camp, no vehicle in those days. Father Rosendo used to take everything he needs in a box and holy water in a bottle. Father put on that purple thing round his neck to do the baptism. Then he did the readings all out of his book in Latin; everything was in Latin, nothing else. The old people just sit down in the camp on the ground, no chairs; that's good enough. Whichever way we find them, that's good enough for old people. When they were baptised, the water was poured over their head out of the bottle and it went in their face, but Father wiped it off. We all say prayers, all in Latin, but now I forget what we said.

After, when he finished, we sit there and talk and Father, too. At lunchtime he said we better go and we left. Somebody from the camp went and picked lunch up at the mission and took it back to the old people in the camp; that happened each day.

Sunday we had two church services, one early and the other one a bit later. We altar boys took turns. We used to have three priests at different altars at the same service. One at the main altar, the others at the small altars. There was no service on Saturdays like we have now in Kalumburu.

A lot of people used to go to church Sundays very early about six o'clock, and the church was always full at both services. First service was for nuns and others who had to go and cook breakfast. When that service finished, we wait outside and then go in for second one, children and adults. The girls and boys from the dormitory used to go to the last service, except when we wanted to go fishing, then we go to the first one; then go fishing.

In those days church service was in Latin. That changed about—wait yet, nearly 1967 or '68. 'Til then, the whole service was in Latin from start to finish. Latin was all right. People didn't worry about it, they understood what the service was to them. They accepted Latin, nobody complained. Every Sunday adults used to go to the catechism class and the Fathers' tell 'em what the words mean. Children learn that in school from the nuns, but not the big people.

In those days, there was no sermon, only Holy Communion; even first and second reading we didn't have. Organ music we did have, an old organ made in Germany. That organ was donated by the German government to the mission because Kalumburu people rescued two German pilots after their plane fall down on the coast. One priest used to play it and Brother. Later, when the nuns came, they taught the girls, Liduvina, Regina, and my cousin that belong to David Maraltadj sister. Her father got killed by that aeroplane accident in Kalumburu.

Before I came to the mission Father Thomas was superior. He translated that Latin into Gunin language, my language, and he put it all in a book. He studied our language and put 'em Latin into our language, so people could understand. I remember that book, I seen it, should be still there. Must find out what happened to it. It was hand-written in ink—English on one side and language on the other. The book was very seldom used. When I was there Father Boniface read it for the people in catechism class. It explain everything. Church service was never taken in Gunin, that was only used outside church. It was for the old people that couldn't come to church. The book was thick enough, it had Bible stories in it, you know? Well, all that was written in language, about a husband and wife in the garden and eat the forbidden fruit. Most people did understand the Bible stories. They thought they were good stories. Some people didn't like it; some people didn't want the religion. We were raised on the mission, so we know about the religion.

We never thought about what the mission was teaching us. At that time most people like to be in the mission, no matter who they were. Some like to go walkabout, go away, stay in the bush. Some didn't bother to get up to go to service on Sundays. People used to be happy in those days, not now. The life was good itself but sometimes things go wrong and it changes. People like the mission because they got tobacco and food and medicine. People who live in the bush still had to hunt and that is work, too; if you don't hunt you die, that's why life in the mission was more easy for everybody.

At Forrest River Mission, they had the Anglican Church there and the service was always in English. English was more better, everyone understands. It's like everybody being together then with the language they all understand—that's good.

We had weddings in the church. That was pretty good in a lot of ways, how they dressed up like husband and wife. The mission provided the clothes, white socks and ties, dress and suits, good clothes. The nuns keep the clothes there; one side of the cupboard marked *Weddings*. When wedding finished clothes have to be returned. Mission organised wedding dinner for family; one month before a notice was put on the church door about the wedding. Many people could read then.

At funerals nothing was organised, no food or cup of tea, nothing. That's still the same today. We didn't have any special clothes for funerals in those days; just ordinary clothes what you go to church in. The black and white clothes which Aboriginal people wear now at funerals just come in lately, we didn't have that in those days. First I seen white woman wear black when their husband die, at that old church in Kununurra. First time I seen that I didn't know why they do that, it reminded me of the priest. Sometime they wear black, too.

When we get first Holy Communion that was the time we dressed up white, me and Barbara Waina, we were the smallest that time and we had it one Christmas night. We must be the same age we two. We went to church at midnight and she and I was wearing white things, and I had a tie first time. I was about ten years old. After the service, every Christmas night, the dormitory children had a bit of a party, just cakes and fruit. It was held in the convent and the families didn't come. The adults went home after the service to sleep.

We understand about religion, what we were taught, like going to church keep you out of trouble, it helps against the bad things, the evil, help you make a good life. You feel it in your body. I know some people don't believe.

In 1996 I lived in Kalumburu for almost a year. The church has changed; it's empty mostly now, most people not interested, they don't go to church. I don't know why they don't bother to go, they just don't like to. I think when it was a mission they were made to go to church, but now there's independence in the community from the mission. The mission buildings are still there like before, but mission don't run Kalumburu any more, the council is supposed to.

When I came back I feel a bit strange. The church look the same as when I left in the 1960s, only older, and inside nearly falling down. The priest faces the people these days in the service. Before he always face the altar. I think I prefer him face the people. Long time ago the service took much longer too, shorter is easier. Now the mission is just like a parish in town and the priest goes out to the stations sometime; the missionaries didn't do that.

I go to church now whenever I feel like it. Most of the time I don't really go to church much because in town it's different. It's not like in the mission when everybody used to live together, and go to church together. Then we are with everybody and you are all there. In town, the other Kalumburu people are usually not there and even if they come to town, most don't bother to come to church. They go straight to drink and spend the money because they can't find drink anywhere else in their community, so they go to town. They only go to church when they're in Kalumburu. Some people do good things because it's part of their nature. You don't have to go to church to be good. I live away from Kalumburu now and I go to church sometime, at Christmas and for funerals.

Mission discipline

When people do wrong thing on the mission, punishments (what) they used to get is flogging with the whip. They called it discipline I think. Married men were flogged when they run away with 'nother woman. They used to go in the bush for months, tribal way, they used to do that, run away with 'nother woman for long time.

Long ago, before the mission was put up, when men run away with 'nother wrong skin woman, they got speared; both man and woman, no mercy in those days. Later, under the mission, married men were only allowed one wife, but some still run off with 'nother one. Even when a man was not married in the mission church but married the tribal way, still an' all he got a flogging, because they allowed to have one wife only, not two or more like before.

In our tribal way, man can have more wives, but second one must not already have a husband. They go away to the bush, man and woman. Might be he had 'nother wife before. He kept that one but want to go away with 'nother one. They disappear about one or two months, or weeks. The first wife is looked after by other family members, that was all right. When they come back they used to have a fight. Might be man and woman's family fight because sometime they go away sneaking, so no one knows. When they come back they used to have a fight. Also, woman and woman used to fight, the first wife fight with the new one. After that they become friends then. Well, that's how it was. The women use a stick for their fight. The first wife fights the new one for stealing her man. When they break up the fight, that's the end. In my days, men only had two wives.

On the mission, some people married wrong way, they married wrong skin, not straight one, you know. They were all single people before, the young ones in the mission, in dormitories, boys in one, girls in 'nother. When people grow up and see each other, they may say, 'Maybe I have this one or that one.' Men would ask the girl first if she wanted to marry him. Men thought: well, I haven't got a straight one, I can't find a straight one, might as well I marry this wrong one. Then they go to the Father and ask when they can get married. Even I could have married the wrong woman there because there was no straight one for me, you see.

Straight one is by the tribes, you know, wrong one is a bit by the side, and then the children come wrong, too. There were not enough people in Kalumburu when we were in the mission. It all depends who was there. Men work full time on mission, but when food supply ran out mission send 'em on holiday in the bush, along the sea or Pago, or Gibb River or Keranji. People cannot marry close relation, they marry from 'nother tribe—Kwini get married to Kulari side, they marry opposite like this, that's supposed to be proper way. People on the mission could only meet others when they go on holiday or walkabout. It was a bit hard too at that time because woman didn't like to move from place to place.

Men didn't care about the floggings. Father used to call 'em, father used to ask people 'Has he come back?' The man would then be called to the mission, and then he got the flogging. The men never talk about it, they know they've done a wrong thing, and then it would be finished.

The man wanted to go back and finish off his troubles, he felt guilty so he came back to the mission after a while. He's satisfied, he ran off, and when he came back he want to settle everything, go back to the woman he married before. No carrying on with the 'nother one any more, the matter is finished then. Lots of people got floggings.

I don't think the women who run away like that got any children out of it; people just didn't have children in the mission in those days. All the men came back to their married wives. If the woman was already married and she just came back to her husband after running away with 'nother man, husband gave her a hiding and then finish. Then they respect each other again. The men feel guilt about giving them hiding, and so it's all right after. No more then . . . finished.

For the flogging they had to kneel down and they get flogged on the back. People had no shirt on. They got it on the bare back. They only had working trousers on. We saw the flogging from a little distance from outside the dormitory. The floggings took place outside the stone building, that was so everybody could see. When we saw it, we didn't look long, we turn our face away or go away. We said nothing. We were scared it might happen to us like that, we were frightened. I could only think of being scared, nothing else.

My brother Martin got a flogging once 'cause he slept with a woman. He left the mission that same night. He said to me, 'I don't want to stay here any more.' When Martin was a boy, he was late to church once and the priest tied him up with a dog collar round his neck and chained him to the mango tree all day. You can ask the old people, they know. He would have been very young still because that happened when mission was at Pago still, before it moved to Kalumburu.

I only got hit with the strap or cane on the hands. One day, after the service, I got into trouble for drinking altar wine. I was altar boy at the same time. I was changing in the sacristy, and then I drink wine what was left over in the glass, just a little bit. I want to know what it taste like. It taste pretty strong. I didn't like it. We didn't know what wine tasted like in those days. When the nuns came to do the church cleaning, they see the wine glass empty, they knew wine was left over after service, so before breakfast they gave me the cane. They said, 'Did you drink the wine?' I said 'Yes.' They could smell it on my breath anyway. They were angry and shouted, 'That's wrong to drink wine,' and I got hit with the cane. They already had the cane ready. They hit me twice on both hands. My friends just laughed and I laughed, too, properly. Sisters whacked us on the hands, hard enough to hurt but I never saw anyone cry.

People were mostly good in those days. Sometimes they also got flogged when they fight with the spear, people were violent now and then; that was their way. People not used to be close together in one place all 'e time. Much of their life had changed then from what it was like in the bush before missionaries came. I think there was a flogging every few weeks. I don't remember seeing much of the men after they bin flogged. We children lived quite separate from the rest of the people; we only went to the camp when we had permission to leave the mission compound. There was no shop to go to in those days either. People got fed by the mission. Children ate in the dormitory, not with everyone. We had small dining room in the dormitory. We didn't mix with anybody unless we went out of the mission.

The camp was a place next to the mission where people lived in corrugated iron huts put there for them. There they used to fight sometime and Father went there, sometime with Brother, to do the flogging. Father didn't like people fighting with the spear, he was aware that somebody might get killed and then there'd be trouble with police. Father used to tell 'em, 'Don't fight with a spear, you get a flogging if you do, you can keep spear for hunting but not for fighting.'

Many people lived outside the mission grounds in their own Kwini or Kulari camps, but nobody got flogging there.

We grew up with the flogging. We got beaten when we were small, when we made noise. Before, Aboriginal people killed each other in the bush, they knew what trouble and violence was. They used to flog each other with the stick in the bush and they fight to protect themselves, too. They had to accept the white man in the mission because missionaries feed 'em with tobacco and flour and sugar, and cook proper meals for them every day—they had to get fed for working. 'Nother way, people respect the missionaries that time, 'cause for a while it was the only place where they got work and food and clothing.

My father kept out of the mission most of the time, he was independent. Only now and then he worked there. People could go to the bush if they wanted but they didn't leave, because they had family in mission, and they couldn't take the children away with them. Only when holiday time came and Father Superior said, 'You can go on holiday,' then they could all go. The mission didn't allow them to take their children out at other times. I see paper in the archive in Perth now that show how Aboriginal children became what they call "wards of the state", once they live in dormitory. Our people didn't realise that back in those days. They couldn't read, many just put their fingerprint on the paper where signature was s'posed to be. They wouldn't have understood what it all meant, none of us did. It's only now that I find out.

Children lived in the dormitory all the time. Sometimes people left without the children, they knew they were looked after. Only later it was, Mr Tilbrook from Welfare, he was the one who say children should be better off with their own parents, so mission then built houses for all the families in the 1960s. Lotteries Commission gave money to build new houses. Once children were no more in the dormitory, the families could leave altogether but most stayed.

Sometime our people did stand up against the missionaries. I hear my eldest brother Henry—same father but from different mother—don't remember what he did or what his punishment was, but I was told one of the priests pointed a gun at him. Henry got the gun and broke it. He passed away long time now.

One day, one of the nuns tied a woman by her hands to a convent post. One of our men who'd been hunting came back and when he heard that, he got an axe, went to the mission compound and cut the rope with an axe and let the woman free. Three men, the priest and Brother and 'nother one wanted to catch him, but he grabbed their heads together and held 'em tight so they couldn't move. Only after a while, he let them go. He was big and strong, he got hold of them and they never moved. Then he just walked off. They didn't dare do anything to him because he was big and very strong.

People used to be punished a lot so they could become good and civilised. I never see a white person flogged. They were the ones who had the power. The flogging only worked the opposite way and Aboriginal people were on the opposite side.

Later the floggings stopped. People were punished in other ways, like they were sent to the bush, or given no tobacco. When they didn't want them there, the superiors banned some people for years from Kalumburu. The mission had a lot of power.

Proper wife
he kill 'im there

Back somewhere in the 1960s, we got the news in the mission this old man was coming into Kalumburu later on, in three or four days. I was a young man then.

After the mail plane landed usual time, we always watch to see who was coming. Later on, when the vehicle was coming straight into the compound of the monastery, we saw this old man and his wife and two children—they were very small—get off the vehicle. We were standing close enough to see it all. First time I heard about this old man was when Father Rosendo told the big people, one time in the evening, when we were sitting down outside. I was quite young that time. Later I used to hear about it again now and then.

For long time, many years this man has bin away. He went away very young. By the time he came back, he seen the place had changed a lot. He was taken away during the war time, that was when people were living at Tingun Paddock (away from the mission buildings, where people had moved temporarily for safety during WWII). That's still a long time ago. It was at the time Father Rosendo was superior and when the old man come back, he still saw Father Rosendo, who was also old then.

The old man wasn't very strong. He was a tall man with very white hair, you know, thin and long he was. First time I see a bloke own a gun. People never had a gun then, people were allowed to use mission guns for hunting and, after, put it in the monastery when we come back. A twelve–gauge the old man had. We were told he had a licence an' later on, we saw he had money, too. I saw money first time when I was in Wyndham hospital in 1959. I was about nineteen then. In Kalumburu, we never see money 'til later.

When he saw Father Rosendo again, the old man cried because he was so happy to be back. He never put his foot on the ground in Kalumburu for long time. He was a Kwini man, my tribe. The wife was middle-aged maybe, the children were only that high, one bigger, the other one carried. Mother was nursing in her arm. One side she was blind. They brought swags and they stayed there. The mission built a cottage for them later.

This old man brought real money then. Brother used to order rations for him from Wyndham. They came with the mail plane. He used to get flour, sugar and tea, and other things. There was no shop there in the community. The mission fed everybody. Later, people saw he used to get lot of things and after a while, the mission ordered things and he bought his supplies from them.

He was away long time because he killed his first wife for a start, proper wife he had. He used to live in the mission and he was married in the church. He was pretty young too, but he was among the first to marry there in the mission. First mob to marry in church was Mary Pandilo. Mission said men who marry in the church could only have one wife, no more.

One day, husband and wife went to Laoar Creek with three or four women for company. They went to get 'em water lilies, they dig that, cut it and eat it later on. The other women went back to mission, only those two left. Later on, he did something with the spear; he killed her near the water there. No one knew. When they were together alone, the old man went and spear her. The old man did it himself and then hide her, buried her in a hollow place under a rock, cover her with leaves and soil, so that's bin help 'im, and he put stones on it.

Then he went to see Father Rosendo and ask him for tea, flour and sugar, maybe not on the same day, but soon after, because when they do something, they run away quick. He told Father Rosendo his wife had run away to Kingana. Father Rosendo couldn't believe him and said, 'Your wife wouldn't do that,' but he gave him what he wanted to get him out of the way, so he could look around and check all those creeks there.

They found his tracks and the body, the foot was sticking out. He did it in a hurry, I think, that's why the foot was sticking out, and they find a bit of blood fell dripping on the rocks. So Father Rosendo went there and Brother ring up, see. They ring up to the police and then the police came. It took 'im several days.

The police came from Wyndham on horseback with two trackers. They had brought spare horses, they always did, one to carry the packs and others for riding. The police went to Kingana to look for him and they found him. He wasn't hiding. The police came suddenly, and he was with the other woman, by that time. I only know they got him and the police told him, 'I don't think you need a wife, you come with us.'

He had chains around the neck and they came back to Kalumburu. I think he may have walked all the way to Wyndham; I'm not sure. They made old Lumpia walk to Wyndham one time, the old man who speared that *kartiya* that raped his wife. Prisoners always walk, no prisoners ride, they always walk. Police ride. When he was in jail in Wyndham, the old man stayed there 'til they had a court. That's where the trial was. The judge sentenced him to life in prison. They said this old man must not return to Kalumburu, never go back to Kalumburu. If he was released, he must not return there. Mission requested that.

Before mission time, the relations of the woman, if they was speared, would get back at the one who speared her. He killed that one, so the family of the other would come and kill him, squaring him up. That was the rule; no trial, square him, that was it. White man way you still go for a long time against this one and that one. Before, if people can't kill the right person, well, they kill one of the family and that would still make it all square. They go mainly for right one, but white man way, you're still in big trouble. You go to the prison. Aboriginal law you get killed because you take a life away from the other person, but that be the end then. Once the two finished that is the end, no more then, people don't think about it any more.

The old man was taken away to Fremantle. Later, they let him go and he came to 'nother place and got a job as a police boy then, and he got 'nother wife. After good while, when he was old, he went back to Kalumburu, when he couldn't work any more. So finally he did come back.

Welfare ring up to the mission say, 'This old fellow is free, he wants to go back there.' Mission said, 'All right he can come back.' Father went and asked people, 'The old man is coming back here'— not asking, he was telling them. People wasn't asked in those days, the mission had the power to bring him back. They said he's coming back.

White man make decision anyway, because they made the rules, just like a station manager, who tells others what to do. White people say we didn't make any progress, so other people come and improve things. They make business and have the power then. That progress means nothing for us. We just have to take it. The white people made progress, but we lost because of that. We mostly lost our land, the ways our people live together, proper way. We used to do what we like before, nobody tell us what to do. White people progress make us go backward. Nowadays our people are mostly poor when before we had everything. Only few Aboriginal people have good things. In those days we couldn't tell 'em, we couldn't turn around. We had no voice then. When the white people come, we had a voice, but voice wasn't loud enough. White people gun was more loud.

It was long and gone what happened to the old man's first wife. All her family is dead now. So when he came back, he settled there and he liked the place, even his 'nother wife. She was not from there, but she was happy to be in Kalumburu, and she died there. People were very happy to see the old man. He came back because all was forgotten, otherwise they could have done something to him. Good enough he had the punishment.

Making the road to Kalumburu and a very bad accident

When I grew up, it was the time Father Boniface was superior. Later on, in 1953 or 1954, when Father Basil was superior, the government sent out a surveyor team to look for a place where they can build a road from Wyndham to Kalumburu. There was no road built before. In those days when the police went on regular patrol around the Kimberley, they had to follow the trackers, because they knew the way through the bush and the white people didn't.

John Morgan was the surveyor. Mounted Police Constable, Laurie Shaw, left Wyndham with a pack of supplies and donkeys and mules and they carried everything. They had with them two Aboriginal men from Moola Bulla settlement out from Halls Creek, young Duncan and Ned. They surveyed for the road from Gibb River to Kalumburu about 1954, which I remember a little bit about.

The surveyors went in front and mark the trees with white paint or ribbons. A day's journey behind came the second team, with a bulldozer and a grader. In that team, they had three big trucks and they carried fuel supplies, food, water and swags. Old deaf fellow, Scotty Salmon, who lived in Keranji, was leading the second team, following the marked trees. The bulldozer came behind and cleared the pathway with the grader, both work together. The men carried special dry meat and tin stuff. They live rough and tough. Nowadays we are spoilt, we carry everything with esky full of ice and Engel fridge that work on a car battery.

In the end, they all came to Kalumburu when the road was finished, as far as there, they couldn't go any further. That road is now the Gibb River Road. Tourists like to go on it now, and it's still not sealed. Still, today in the Wet, no one can get through for many months because the rivers rise high and the road becomes a bog. That road team must have started after the Wet. They reached the mission in winter still. The road is a dirt track, good enough for vehicle to pass through and it was very exciting when we heard the road was completed. For the first time people from the outside world could drive to the most isolated mission in the Kimberley.

When the surveyors arrived in the mission, we were out in Pago with the nuns, who were soon leaving for New Norcia. Father Basil received a message on the radio that the surveyors were in Kalumburu.

The people who built the road, stayed in the mission for three weeks. Our feeling was very good because first time we see so many outside people at once. When they went back, we never saw them again. They went to Carson River Station, about twenty kilometres south of Kalumburu, which was built already by Jack Eagleston, the only white man we knew then not living in the mission.

The year before that road was finished, in about 1953, there was a bishop came from England to visit Kalumburu on his way to New Norcia. He wanted to go early in the morning to Wyndham or Darwin to get 'nother plane to go to New Norcia. The pilot slept in Kalumburu that night. The arrangement was made that me and Francis and one boy called Ferdinand, go to the old camp there to tell Laurie Waina and Willie Maraltadj, David's father, to bring the old Ford 20 Cut Weight* in the morning.

Willie Maraltadj and Laurie Waina had to bring the truck around in the morning, to take the Bishop to the airstrip. Brother Andrew and Father Basil and 'nother Bishop from Darwin visiting Kalumburu, went with them. It was small plane, a Cessna, like Ord Air charter planes now, single engine. The pilot was Ralph

* Cut: local parlance for cwt: hundredweight, 1/20th of a ton — the truck was a one-tonner

Thomson. He was young. He was from Darwin—no Kununurra in those days, only Wyndham and Darwin. Ralph Thomson must be in Darwin area now, I don't know.

Laurie Waina drove, but when the others all got out on the airstrip, Father Basil was sitting in the cabin waiting with one other person for the plane to take off, sitting on the passenger side. Willie Maraltadj was standing behind the cabin on the truck. When the plane was loaded up, it took off on that mission side runway where we always take off, the usual one; when you take off you go over Malinjarr, that side. There were two runways built in the shape of a cross; they crossed each other in the middle. The pilot asked Laurie to park the truck on one runway, with its headlights facing across the way the plane was going to take off, across that runway. The pilot told Laurie to park there because of a rough spot in the runway and he wanted to get up in the air before he got to it. The pilot used the truck lights to guide his plane. There was no other light on the airstrip at all. Only much later, they used kerosene lamps to guide the plane to land in the dark. We boys light the lamps when we hear the plane come.

That morning, I was going to be altar boy and waited for Father Basil to come back from the airstrip for service. I remember it was very cold and I was freezing. It was winter, in July, the coldest month. Finally, we heard the plane take off— we could see the lights on in the wing. We heard it take off with all its might and, all of a sudden, we heard a bang, like it hit something and from there, the engine stopped. We knew something wrong but they had no other truck to go and have a look. Then we see a bloke run from the airstrip with a torch. Laurie, he came and he told people. He told David Maraltadj's mother how it happened.

Later, we heard the pilot couldn't see in the front because it was heavy fog. The plane hit the truck. The propeller cut the roof of the cabin of the truck right off, and Willie Maraltadj died instantly. Father Basil got hit in the chest as the landing wheel from the plane came through.

Laurie Waina was off the truck and rolled over on the ground when the plane hit. Brother Andrew had gone for toilet in the bush, so he didn't get hit. Only two people were in the truck cabin. Willie Maraltadj was standing on the back of the truck. The other person in the cabin wasn't injured, only Father Basil.

All of a sudden, we hear people cry everywhere, and then Laurie came to the mission. We were all standing around and said, 'What happened?'

'An accident happened, Father Basil is half dead, wounded by the wheel. Willie Maraltadj died instantly, the plane hit him on the truck,' Laurie said. Everyone cried. I cried for him too, you know.

The propeller hit him on the side of the head and he died instantly. Propeller break the cabin and all. They went and collected another vehicle. One white bloke from the mission drove it and he and Father Rosendo collect the body. There was a nun who was the clinic Sister, and they brought Father Basil back to the clinic and then they all wait for 'nother plane to come to pick up the injured person. Father Basil was on a stretcher and next day he was flown to Wyndham and stayed away a long time.

I don't know about other people, but I still remember it each time I go to Kalumburu.

Later on, they cut all the broken bits off and used the truck without it, cut it all off, leave it open, no windscreen, nothing. Then Jack Eagleston from Carson River Station bought it for £500, I think. So that morning everybody cried. People couldn't stop crying for a long time.

Maybe I was about thirteen or fourteen then. We used to get up about half past five. It was still dark when we get up. Earlier that morning they start the generator up for the lights, the Brother did that, we had it going 'til about nine or ten o'clock at night. That Bishop and some other people from England came. Well, they only stayed a few days, and the English Bishop was telling us children stories about seeing three stars together. He said, 'We can see that from England, but we can't see the Southern Cross from England.' Night-time he came to talk to us outside the convent. There was a light on and seats. After supper he used to talk to the children.

Willie Maraltadj was a young man. He was mechanic, truck driver, barge driver, stockman, a bit of everything. He was married to David's mother, Aunty Nellie. He had two daughters and two sons, but when that thing happened, the family was outside the mission, in the camp, not far. Nellie Maraltadj had three children then. One girl, she died small because they were eating poison turtle. The other daughter, Irene, was playing the piano later but when she was about twelve or thirteen, she almost drowned in the Running Creek, when it was still a bit high after the Wet. After that she was ill and she died in Derby hospital.

Aunty Nellie's mother was related to my father, who was her uncle. My brother-in-law was her eldest boy and already in the dormitory. Irene was second and David was third. Later came Clement from different father and born much later, in Father Sanz time. This was Father Basil time.

Aunty Nellie stayed in the dormitory after the accident, together with the children. Willie Maraltadj had one sister, Dolores, from one mother. Dolly was married already and her husband was there. Later he went to leprosarium. When husband away, the women were kept in the dormitory, so they don't muck around with anyone. That was a rule of their husbands. Mission was trying to help them look after the children.

Father Rosendo was in charge of the mission then. Wait yet; later on a CIB and another policeman came to find out about the accident. Police took reports for two days. After that, they left and Father Basil went to hospital in Perth. We never hear no more about the accident from anywhere. People talk about it among themselves and I think they blamed the pilot.

Father Rosendo got insurance for falling off the roof some time before, he told me himself. He said, 'Insurance paid me £300' Maybe it was £500. I don't remember the exact amount. Father Rosendo was hurt and he was paid insurance for the accident when he worked for the mission, but Aboriginal people did not. Father Rosendo had arm trouble after the accident. Father Boniface was superior when Father Rosendo fell from the roof. I know for a fact that the mission building was insured for £5000. I think the family should get compensation for the accident because it was very terrible, and Willie Maraltadj was working for the mission at the time of the accident. He was my cousin/brother and a young man then and it wipe out his whole life. He bin working as mechanic, barge driver on the lugger, and as a stockman. The mission insured the buildings and they couldn't insure the Aboriginal people that bin working hard there.

The aircraft accident happened about 1953. Father Rosendo fell off the roof before then. Mission was insured too, during the war, it says there in the Kalumburu War Diary. The insurance paid for mission staff, but not for Aboriginal people when they had accident, they didn't know their rights at all in those days. I don't think anyone insured them and they didn't know themselves what to do. They didn't know what bad things could happen to us. Willie Maraltadj was killed after Father Rosendo was paid insurance for his accident.

In 1996, Father Sanz told us in New Norcia that there was no insurance for anybody. In the late 1950s, Lesley French, who was raised on the mission, worked on the mission outstation called Jiliowei, and he tried to fix a truck that had stalled. The carburettor caught fire and burned him so badly they thought he would die. My brother-in-law went on a horse at night all the way from Jiliowei to Kalumburu to get help for him. And he got nothing from any insurance. Still today he got big scars from the burns.

Native hospital

First time I bin on an aeroplane was when I was sick and had to go to the Native Hospital in Wyndham. They put me on a small plane in Kalumburu. I used to see a lot of planes fly but I never went myself.

I had to lie down on a stretcher, I was that sick. Doctor gave me bit of injection so I wouldn't feel the pain. My left foot was swollen. I had pus in it and the pain went all the way to the groin. I had injections before in the mission for polio and sickness.

The plane was called Dove. It was the Royal Flying Doctor plane and doctor and nurse came with me. This was the first time I left Kalumburu since I came there as a small child.

When I was in the air, I feel movement all the time and I was a little bit worried about what might happen next. We had strong wind, too, a bit rough, 'cause it was December, hot weather time and with the Wet coming soon. I was a bit happy too because I thought I might see some of my family there in Wyndham. Only had my brothers and sisters left and I didn't see much of them in the mission. They were mostly in Forrest River Mission or Wyndham.

First they let me sleep a bit on the flight, then nurse said, 'We'll be landing soon' and we were in Wyndham. From the airstrip, doctor took me to the Native Hospital and we got there 'bout sunset time. The hospital is a bit outside the town, where Joorook Ngarni Resource Centre is now.

Orderly came, Aboriginal bloke—he bin dead long time now. He took me to have a shower and gave me crutches to help me walk. Sister put bandages on my foot. They were very good nurses in those days. They were all white and they work straight away when someone comes in. I met old Ernest, he work around hospital too, and I asked him if he could let my brother Brian know that I am here. Next morning Brian came. I last saw him in Kalumburu when I was a child. He come and shake hand and talk—he never drink in those days. He'd come from Forrest River to see me, and he had to go back on the barge the next day. I was glad to see him.

'Nother one was there, too, my other brother, Gwen's husband, Martin. He came in the boat from Forrest River too, to see me. You see it's easier for people from Forrest River to come to Wyndham than to go to Kalumburu. I was really happy I could see him again.

I stay at the hospital for two weeks. For X-ray I had to go to 'nother white hospital in the doctor car, and I had lunch there. They had to build two hospitals in Wyndham because the white people didn't like to be in same place as us Aboriginal people. First they had only one hospital for white people. When Aboriginal people get sick, they bin treated in the missions, and if mission staff didn't know what to do, they call for doctor to fly out. Sometime doctor said he's too busy and can't come. Once in Kalumburu, one woman got very, very sick. She just born her first baby that time. Doctor said on the phone to give her some pills but she got worse. Mission call doctor but he still too busy, so mission sent the woman to Darwin hospital. Doctor there said she had meningitis. That's very serious, you can easily die. Lucky she survived.

In about 1933, Forrest River Mission sent one woman to the only white hospital in town to have a baby. Just before that, there was other sick Aboriginal people start to come to that hospital. White people didn't like to see Aboriginal people there, so some white people got together and complain to authorities in Perth. Letters went to Medical Department and even Lands Department in the city. Medical Department write back to Dr Hungerford in Wyndham and ask him to please explain why Aboriginal maternity case was admitted to that ward. The matron of the hospital wrote to the Medical Department in Perth, 'At the Mission they have their own hospital … whereas I have no accommodation for them here. It is out of the question, I suppose, to admit them to the Maternity Ward, and no other part is registered, nor suitable to deal with them. I consider the hospital is becoming a cheap boarding place for Forrest River Natives.'

I know Forrest River Mission didn't have a proper hospital. That's why a small town like Wyndham had two hospitals 'cause the white people didn't like to be treated in same place as our people.

Well, when I was there, our Native hospital was pretty good. It was steel building, cyclone proof and very solid, but much smaller than the white hospital. Our hospital had section for men and 'nother one for women. Inside it had twelve beds one side and twelve on the other, and curtains between them. Nurses were all white; you didn't expect Aboriginals in such jobs then, only white people. Aboriginal people didn't have much education in those days; there was no money for training. They could only be employed as a worker or cleaner, on the wharf or on stations.

When I first come to the hospital, I was a bit lonely, only some beds were occupied. Big mob had bin but all left now. I only met one bloke there from a station. I wished I could be back in Kalumburu. There we used to be with everybody all the time, among a lot of people and we all know each other.

One day, doctor said, 'We're taking you back,' and when we took off I sat in a seat this time. Plane stopped at Forrest River Mission. I'd not bin there for many years. This plane we come on is called "the doctor run", 'cause that's when doctor come regular to isolated communities and he got to come by plane. They still do that now. I walk around a bit seeing friends and family. Enid, Brian's wife, had the first girl then, Sylvia. My sister-in-law Gwen was there, too. Lot of people came to see me and mission Sister made tea and we had sandwiches and cake. Some people said, 'Do you remember this place, you came here when you bin small?' I couldn't remember.

In the afternoon when doctor finished with everybody, we flew to Kalumburu. I couldn't talk to anyone on the plane because there's too much noise from the engine. I was excited looking through the window at the country and had no idea how far Kalumburu is. I was a bit scared too, first time I sit on a plane. Last time I bin sick and lie down. Later one of the Sisters told me Kalumburu is ahead of us. Finally, we circled round and down and I see the river and the buildings and the landing strip. I saw Brother Dominic coming to the airstrip in the Landrover to meet the doctor.

Back in the dormitory, I had a rest because my head was going round and round. My ears was paining from the noise in the plane. Later, at night-time, I was all right again.

I was thinking, one day I go back to Wyndham and look at the place and work. I didn't see very much this time, 'cause I bin sick and in a hospital. I was a bit homesick too and glad to be back in Kalumburu. It was still the good old days in Kalumburu when we were there with everybody all the time and that was good. When you go out you all alone, you have to look after yourself.

Sailing trip

Back in about 1953, we boys went on a trip for a holiday break from the mission. We were in the dormitory at that time. I was sixteen then. Father Basil was in charge of the mission from 1952 to 1955. Father Sanz became superior then, he was the last one 'til 1982, when the Kalumburu community became independent from the mission. Father Basil liked taking us on holiday. He took us on the mission lugger *Myrtle Olga*. It was repaired in Darwin and it had sails. It was pretty big and used for cargo. There were three or four cabins underneath the deck, an engine room, radio room and one with bunks in three rows.

The people who went with me were Leslie French, his brother Raymond, Placid, and my brother-in-law, John Maraltadj. Big people was Louis Karadada, Jackie Lefthand, Francis Waina, Jeffery (Sylvester father) and Alan, (Karina father) and Peter Waimundo, that's all. They were young married men. Only the men came. There was Bob, one white bloke from Darwin, who used to work in Truscott. His 'nother name was Philip. Bob was a pretty short bloke and he had a big beard and a hump on his back.

We helped with the loading; we were willing to do anything. We took two pairs of shorts and T-shirts. All had our names sewn on them, nuns used to do that and all had different colours. One good pair of shorts we had to go to church.

The Aboriginal men all knew how to handle the lugger. We kids had no responsibilities. Old Louis used to be in charge of us boys on the lugger. We started at lunchtime and first went from

Longangi to Truscott. We take everything—flour, sugar, dry meat and corned meat, baked beans, tea, powdered milk and tomatoes. The meat was salted in a bag; dry, it could be taken anywhere. It was no camp oven in those days so we took bread tins in case we wanted to make bread. We went for two weeks on that trip, long way we went. We didn't worry about anything.

We went in the dry season from Longangi and it was full tide. We don't use sails, only when the wind comes up. To start the motor, Louis and some others used to wind 'em up underneath. It was a big diesel engine and we need two men to turn the big cranking handle. When the motor started, we all ready, standing there on the deck and then we moved out.

We enjoyed looking around and we sit down in the front on the deck. Louis was a good sailor. He was sailing right through to Truscott then others took over. They told us to keep clear, and where we could sleep and sit. We passed *Kul*, a mighty big mountain. We never went on top, we just passed there.

For me it was the second time I went to Truscott, it took to nearly sunset to reach there. We anchored near the beach and took a dinghy to the shore, wandered around and then returned to the lugger to sleep. It was in a wooden dinghy and carries about twelve people. We had no life jackets, we didn't know about them. We were good swimmers.

At night we stay on board. There were mattresses, very small ones, like swag mattresses, laid out on deck but we could also sleep inside the cabin. I sleep on the deck all the time. On deck it was cool in the wind, we need a blanket for cover. We had small army type pillows, which could be folded double. In the morning, old Louis cooked breakfast on a metho burner. You pumped it like a hurricane lamp, put a match to it and—*shhhhhhh*—it lights up.

Early in the morning, when the tide came in, we pulled the anchor up and left. From Truscott, we went with the sail to Troughton Island, long way away in the Timor Sea. Half way to that island you can feel the strong current in the sea. We reached there at sunset time across the open sea. Troughton Island is right outside, you don't hardly see it 'til you come closer and closer. The sea was rough but we went one side where the calm water is. We passed the last bit of mainland, that tip of land we call 'Woolola'. Then we went out to the open sea past this island called Eclipse Island, passed there and to Troughton Island, and we camped round that way. Next day we went to Long Reef. We reached there about lunchtime and anchored.

Long Reef is a big white sandbar, no land, just dry sand and it's high, never covered even at high tide. We anchored there, no land, no stone, nothing growing, no spinifex, no trees, not even mangroves, nothing, just pure white sand. It's pretty high like a mountain, just like an island, about the height of the salt pile in Port Hedland* that big salt, only longer. It sloped down and had beaches on both sides.

They chucked the anchor and the men went hunting for turtles in the dinghy: Louis, Peter, Alan, Jackie Lefthand and Clement's father: Waimundo. They got a spear, a harpoon spear, the ones like you see at One Arm Point (Bardi Community, West Kimberley). They went round and round in the dinghy, then we seen a bloke there dive, and we said, 'Oh, they got one turtle!'

They move quietly, using paddle all the way. The turtle don't mind the noise of the paddle, but with dugong, you can't make a sound, not one sound, they move like the wind. One sound and they're gone. Men stand up in the front of the boat, then dive with the spear to get the turtle. They jump same time as they spear, we seen 'em do it. They got to jump in to get it. If they miss they got to dive to get the spear. Spear is sharp, made of steel. Haven't seen wooden spearhead used, only seen steel one. The turtle tries to get away but the bloke sometime ride on it to control it. You need to be careful because they can bite pretty strong. Men lift 'em up by the side so the turtle can't dive down. The men lift it up by the shell and the people in the boat get it up into the dinghy.

People hunt where there are no crocodiles, but there can be sharks hang around sometime. Crocs are in the mangroves, usually they like the dark shady spots, not right outside in the open water. Shark is the one you got to be careful of, they can smell the blood of anything killed; bloke got to be there with the dinghy. We saw a shark circling then, as they loaded the turtles

* Cargill Salt, Port Hedland, WA: salt storage pile about 8m high

in the lugger. The lugger was higher than the dinghy, so the turtles were tied with rope and pulled up.

We went to Parry Harbour from there looking for a place to camp because it's nice there and calm in the creeks. When we were just ready to move out, we saw the shark again. We started the engine and it was still following. That Bob fired a shot at him and it took off to the open ocean, never come back again.

When we went to the Parry Harbour Creek in the big bay, we took all the turtle meat and cooked it on the beach. Parry Harbour is a beautiful place, rocks and a big mountain and a beach, trees, white gum and others. I don't know if there was water. We brought six or seven 44-gallon drums with water from Kalumburu. One had a tap.

It was late afternoon and we made a big fire on the beach. We boys collect the driftwood on the beach and we also looked for harder wood, for strong white gum. We cook the turtles as the sun was going down. Only Father Basil and Bob and one other man stayed behind on the lugger.

Louis was in charge of us boys and he did cooking for us. He told us lot of stories about how it was when he was young— he knew the place really well. Jackie Lefthand made damper. The turtles were cooked buried in the ashes and with hot stones inside them. They knew when it would be ready to eat. Later, when it was dark, everything was cooked and we ate turtle and damper and drank water. 'This is your turtle, you help yourself,' Louis said. We ate it just like that, we didn't use salt; you don't need salt for seafood. Late night, we went back to the lugger and took the meat back in the shell—it's like a dish—so Father Basil and the others could eat. The parts we didn't cook, we left for dingoes to eat.

That country belongs to the Kulari people, but nobody lived in it when we were there. Louis told us one old woman got lost there once, so the boys were frightened to sleep on the beach. When we were young, we are frightened of anything. We were frightened of that woman's spirit. She lived in that country but her mind was out of order and she wandered away and got lost. We said, 'We better go back on the lugger.'

Every morning we used to take turns watering the deck. Like pearling luggers, you must water it with the seawater so the wood remains hard. Next day, we went back again on land to do fishing. We caught some bluebone. We fished with string line, not nylon, proper white coil, with St Paul written on it. Ordinary fishing line, it was. Oh, they last for long time! It's pretty strong and you put a hook on it, no reel in those days, we had it round a stick or board. We fished off the rocks. Luis went with the fish wire. This is made out of a piece of strong, single mesh wire. The tip is attached to a piece of bamboo, joined with wax from the bush honey. The wax doesn't break because it gets hard when it dries, and even water won't make it break. The bamboo is needed for holding the spear when you throw it. When you miss, the bamboo is the one that make it float in the water, so you can pick it up again.

Louis got a big bluebone off the rocks. He speared it straight through the gills, he got two and gut 'em up and cook it and we eat it there. The ocean is crystal clear there, very clean, no pollution, you can see a long way. The bluebone fish was very big, cooked in the ashes on hot stones on the beach and we turn it over with a stick when it's done on one side.

Then they said, 'We're going to leave tomorrow.' We left that place and sailed to Gibson Point, north west and camped there one night. Gibson Point we just looked around, big bay with big mountain, all covered with trees. We went exploring for two days.

We didn't like to camp at Troughton Island, it was coral reef there. When the tide is low, you cannot go any closer to the island with the dinghy because the reef is exposed. We lived on turtle still. Once it's cooked, it doesn't go bad for a while and there are no flies on the sea. We passed north of Eclipse Islands. The islands were only small, then across to Sir Graham Moore Island. The open sea is rough there in the strong sea breeze. Later on we anchored at Governor Island where we jumped off. It's only straight across from Sir Graham Moore. We took the dinghy to explore right around one of them. We found oysters. They were that big!* I had only one or two, then we went back on board and slept there. Father Basil was talking on the radio to the mission in Kalumburu: 'We're coming in tomorrow,' he told 'em.

* Palm size

47

From there, we sailed to Longangi. By the time we reach Monger Creek we watch the tide, there's a sand bar where we get stuck sometimes. As we were travelling, Father Basil and Louis checked the mangroves for the level of the tide. Father Basil had a tide chart. We drop anchor near the Kul Mountain, wait for the tide to rise, so we won't get stuck on the sandbar.

Lunchtime, we moved in to Longangi. Louis always took the wheel to Longangi. We liked to be back in Kalumburu. We enjoyed the trip but we had enough, see. Tide was coming in full now. When we turned into the bend they slowed the engine down and the boys jumped off and tied the lugger up. There used to be lots of old tyres at the landing to protect the lugger. Laurie Waina came with the truck to pick us up.

When I go to Kalumburu now, I think a lot about Louis Karadada. Warburn Bay is his country. He's a very important person, nobody knows. The younger people don't realise. He took care of us, he told us what is what. He used to teach us a lot, devil dance, and others. He used to go backwards and tell how people used to live. People in Kalumburu now don't realise how important he is and how he was trusted by the mission to drive the boat night-time. He has a lot of sea skills. He used to go from coast to coast before the missionaries were there. He knew how to navigate.

Nowadays, there is not much for old people to do in Kalumburu. In the old days, people would all take notice of them because they used to listen to the old people especially—now they don't any more.

Old people knew where to go

In early 1960s, we wanted to go to Forrest River overland, Francis Waina, Father Sanz, and me. I 'specially wanted to go for that trip to see the bush, but mostly I wanted to see my relations in Forrest River, for that I wanted to go. Father Sanz ask me if I want to come. I said, 'Yes.' He wanted to find a track through the bush for mission cattle. Two old people, one Placid, the other one Murrel, both of them Kwini, also come 'cause they used to walk up and down all the time between Kalumburu and Forrest River. They knew where to go.

Mission want to find a way to get its cattle to Wyndham while the meat works there was still going. Every year, mission do mustering and they had a good number of cattle. Mission wanted to make money from the cattle and they were ready to go. Father Sanz think if the cattle can walk to Forrest River and then go on the barge frol there to Wyndham, is cheaper than sending them all the way on a ship from Kalumburu to the meat works. That's why we went in a four wheel drive to look for a track the cattle might go on.

Landrover been donated by Lotteries Commission and it came by ship. Road to Kalumburu was not properly used yet; vehicles came on a barge, that big one, was already bought by mission before; so the new Commer truck and Landrover came on that. Both brand new, not a bit of rust on them.

We went on our trip in the new Landrover. It had a big tray and it was set up for journey. Driver was Francis and Father Sanz sat in the cabin with him. We three sat in the open back. They had put a proper bench there for us to sit on, nailed to the tray. It was good to look at the places on the way too, because I hadn't bin in the bush much, not so far from the mission. We took food, flour, rice, must a bin that tin food, and some diesel, four gallon small drums, bit of bread, biscuit and cordial, and the waterbag. We didn't have esky in those days, waterbag hang in the front, better than carrying esky or ice, so water won't be too cold.

We drive out through Jiliowei, that is Barton Plain and it start from Drysdale River. There was a bit of a road there already up to that house on Barton Plain Station. It was built by old Peter, Mary Pandilo father, and Laurie Waina and other Aboriginal men in the 1950s. Mission had a lease on that land for a while to raise cattle. We followed that road and camped one night there. The track ended there; no road go any further. Next day we crossed that Drysdale River, then the old men tell Francis where to drive through the bush. Sometime we stand up on the tray to look ahead where the vehicle could go and dodge the rough parts. We tell the driver with our hands, this way or that way. Father Sanz had back trouble, he always must sit in the cabin.

When we come to that Woolumboorwembardoo jump-up, where that road is today going right over the top, we find that hill was too high and too rocky. We couldn't drive round that jump-up. It was a big mountain and we had to clear a path for the vehicle to climb over. We take a hammer and a crowbar to break the rocks. If you want to break anything, crowbar is handy then. We moved rocks away, so we could pass, some we had to break with the crowbar, move it away one side. Nearly the whole day it took us, you know how high it is. Well, that's the jump-up now. When we knock off, Francis start to drive with the four wheel drive and it was easy to climb up. So we had meal there on top, watermelon and meat and bread. From there we drove a bit more and camped somewhere. Just before dark we spotted a *punurr*, a bush turkey. Father Sanz shot it. He had a gun and he was a good shot really.

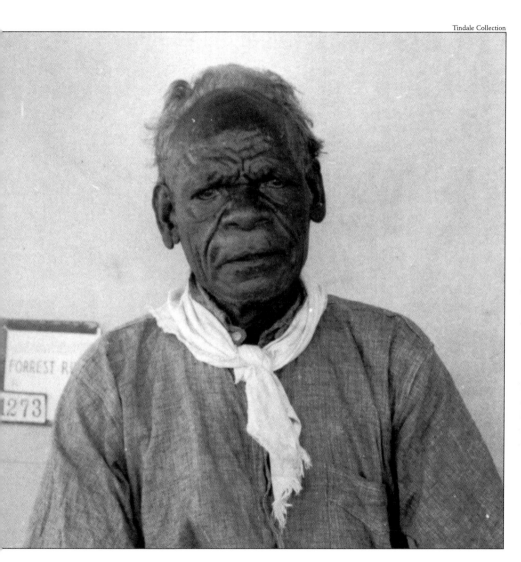

Ambrose's father's brother, Munggoola.
(According to Ambrose, he bears a striking resemblance to his own father)

Boab in the wet, Great Northern Highway near Wyndham

Dancing with decorations—Kalumburu, 1950s

"Now I say people these days don't dance because everything is lost. From the beginning people were dancing all the time, culture was full, that means full of things like our language, our way of life, our Lalai (Dreamtime). They never dance juluroo, kurranganda, jorrmala, yarrami and junba any more because the old people all passed away. With the young generation, everything is lost"

Lining up for tobacco rations, circa 1925, Drysdale River Mission (Drysdale River Mission was the original name for Kalumburu Mission when it was located at Pago, 30km north of its present location)

We cook it the traditional way, Francis and me. We dug a big hole, make a fire and when it's hot we put stone and wood on top. When fire is big the stones get hot. Fire must die down first, and then we put the bird on the hot stones wrapped in gum leaves. More leaves go on top very thick and then soil to cover it all. It take a long time to cook, you know. We cook it when sun was just going down and we can smell it, after a while, when it was cooking. When it was finally ready, we dig it out, put it on fresh gum leaves and eat it. There was plenty for all of us and we had damper an' a tea with it. We really enjoyed that.

We camped there and it was a wonderful night, we heard wild bulls too. There was enough meat for the next day. We carry it in a hessian bag, was very handy, that plastic these days is no good. It was cold weather and we sleep in proper swags, the old type; it had canvas and blankets in it, keep the water out too, same way as stock camp. No mattress but we had blankets to sleep on. Old swag is same green colour as new one, and canvas was good. Old swag had no mattress in it like today, so we use a few blankets instead, that make swag very heavy. We sleep with the fire burning and we manage to keep warm. The Kimberley night can be cold in the dry season.

Next morning, we bumped into the river, the King George. One old man said, 'This is Oomarri a bit higher up'. Francis said the other day that we crossed lower down, not at Oomarri, that's right, that's what the old man said at the time. We crossed one deep creek with all the pandanus there and we got bogged.

I remember it well. I thought it was hard ground but we got bogged in the sand, it was soft. Father Sanz said we can't leave it here, vehicle worth a lot of money, so we work 'til we got it out. The car was in the river; water running. We cut big tree and put rocks underneath. The vehicle was in deep, up to the axle. We dug and dug and put lot of wood there, and big, big stones, then move the vehicle bit backward and bit forward, and finally we got it out, and crossed the river.

We went on. I don't know how far, we see all those big ranges there. We only took one 44-gallon drum diesel and we thought it better to turn back 'cause fuel was low. We wanted to go to Forrest

River Mission and fill up the tank there, but we couldn't get down. The place was a bit too rough, you know how the bush is there, so we came straight back same way. Only we crossed the river somewhere else, didn't get bogged this time. The bush was wonderful in those years; you wouldn't recognise it now. No big fires destroy it yet.

I knew I bin somewhere around the place but only recognise the river. I walk with my family from Forrest River to Kalumburu when I was small, maybe several times, but only recognise the river. I hadn't been back to my country for about fifteen years at that stage. I didn't think so much about my country then, only Forrest River. I wanted to go because my people were there. They were all in Forrest River, though a lot of them were passed away by then already.

When we turn back to Kalumburu, Father Sanz said no way you can get the cattle through there. He said he'll find 'nother way for the cattle. Later he build a cattle yard there at Paloo outside Kalumburu, that race there we saw near Winanghie. He shipped the cattle out that way. Ningle Haritos was a man who sometime work for mission, and Ningle came back from Darwin to ship the cattle out on the barge. A good number of cattle would fit on that. They had to make a few trips, I think. Two trucks can fit on that barge; it was pretty wide and long. St Joseph, it was called, all steel. Someone told me the mission managed to make some money out of the cattle. I don't know—I left the mission soon after that.

Mission labourers

Near Kalumburu there is a place called Truscott. It's really country belong to *Kulari* people and they call it *Anjo*. Truscott was named after Bluey Truscott, a white man. The government put an airbase in that place in the Second World War, and many Aboriginal people from the mission worked there. They were called the mission labourers and they bin working at Truscott airbase without pay. There were lot of people working there, Kularis mainly, and some Kwinis, yeah, mission labourers; that's what they were called and I knew them all.

When government build airbase there, soldiers were stationed in Kalumburu. When I was small I see a lot of soldiers. After mission got bombed, they were all moved to Truscott to build new airstrip there. The Abbott of New Norcia didn't want soldiers there in Kalumburu after the bombing, that's why they had to move out.

The Japanese bombed Kalumburu 'cause it had an airstrip very close to the community. In that raid, two planes came flying over Woraro Hill and straight down across over the mission buildings. That's when the priest got killed, the superior, Father Thomas and the Aboriginal children.

That's why they moved the soldiers to Truscott in 1943 'cause it's a bit further away from Kalumburu. Japanese came the other way, they couldn't see that airstrip, it was camouflaged—they came past Pago, Sir Graham Moore Island, they never bomb that Truscott, they didn't see it.

Country belong to Kulari. They were living there and they were used as messengers by the army. There was no road, nothing, just bush. The people walked along bush tracks to Kalumburu and back. It was rough area, it took 'em about one day, start early in the morning and get there in the afternoon. They'd come out through the Running Creek at Kalumburu. My father was working there at Truscott at that time, too.

The people who work there used to live like kings. They got food, tin food, flour, tobacco. My father used to bring some bread and tin food when he came back—tin meat, fresh meat and everything in hessian bag. They told us stories but I don't remember much. When the war was finished, the army left everything there and went away. Mission got a truck from there; they put it on the barge to bring it across the bay to Kalumburu.

After the war contract was given to one white bloke called Mick Davies, at end of 1950s. He came from Darwin area. We knew him because he comes there now and then. He used to come to Truscott and to the mission a lot, first on a plane, sometime on a boat. His work was to take out all the bullseye mesh* laying down on the airstrip and ship it away. It took a few months.

Well, back in the '50s, Mick Davies came to Kalumburu few times to look for and find things he can collect. He was mostly mechanic, I think; before he own a garage in Darwin, an' a lot of time he used to come here, Father Boniface and Father Sanz time. He was working in the mission too, on the side; bit of help, mechanical work, mission knew him pretty well.

He was given accommodation in return for work. Mick used to ask Father, 'Can I do anything?' Father used to give 'im jobs; I was in the dormitory then. We knew him very well. He speak very good English, he was bit middle-aged and he was a very good man, too. Spare time, he take fencing to Carson Station and to Arugun. I did go with him once, me and three boys, we went with him loading up wire for Arugun, put it up there and then come back. Arugun is where King Edward River joins Carson River. They put up fence line there, because Jack Eggleston had Carson Station, and the fence was Kalumburu boundary next to it. Arugun belonged to mission too, it's past

* Marsden matting

Poteirta Hill, when you pass that Carson River Crossing, well that's Kalumburu fence line that; now is nothing, it all belong to the community.

Later, Mick went back to Darwin for some time, and then work in Truscott in the 1960s. Mission had a barge then, a big one that was used for that Truscott job, and Mick had that contract to take that steel out. Father Sanz and Brother Dominic, they were working there too, keeping an eye on the barge St Joseph and everything. Aboriginal mission labourers went to Truscott on the barge, a whole heap of them. Oh, by golly, lots of people went, some still alive. It was Louis Karadada, Alan (Karina father) and Jeff, (Sylvester father), old Wilson, they all passed away, Basil Djanghara, Robert Unghangho, old Paul Miuron (Dolly's uncle), old Alec, Laurie Waina, Francis Waina—he used to work for Mick all the time there, permanently. Then it was Albert, he became blind late, Albert Wiler, an' old Joe Puruan. My brother wasn't there, but Clement's father, Peter Waimundo, was there. I think Wagan Djanghara was there too. Dangal an' old Dickie Woodmorro worked at stations in the Gibb River area, but old Rankin Karadada was there, too, that's just about all the men in those days from the mission.

I think the work lasted for two months. People live there while they work 'til they finish. They were fed there and they sleep on the beach. It was dry time, Aboriginal people didn't need accommodation, and only Father and Brother sleep on the barge.

People work there, taking the bullseye mesh out from the airstrip, making it lose, sheets got hook to connect each other. Mick had a big truck there. Francis Waina used to drive it. From the airstrip they used to take up the bullseye mesh, load it on the truck and from there it went down to the beach, a distance of about twelve kilometres. It was the first road I seen, it was a bitumen, big pipes and water goes underneath when it cross a creek. On the beach, they heaped it in great piles, and when it was ready, a ship called Isabelle came there.

That ship had mostly Chinese people in it, Chinese crew, that's the first time Aboriginal people from Kalumburu saw Chinese people and chopsticks. They only knew spoon and fork, not chopsticks. First time people see 'em use chopsticks to eat rice, they thought everybody outside the mission used spoon and fork to eat.

They used the barge *St Joseph*, the mission barge, to take the steel from the beach to the ship. The truck had a crane too, and they lay bullseye mesh on the beach so truck could go on the sand with the weight on and not get bogged. Crane was used to load the steel on the barge, but the people stack the mesh on the truck with their hands. The ship was just anchored in the deep water and barge had to go out when tide was right.

All that bullseye mesh went to Darwin with Mick. I don't really know what happened, only hear stories. Mesh was put there by the army, how could people just pull it up and sell it? It was all organised by Mick. Before that Mick went to Kalumburu first collecting copper, battery things and bullet shells, at the same time he went to Truscott; that was after the war. He also took old radiators and bullet shells; he was collecting spent cartridges round the airstrip, one drum full of it. First he took all that copper back to Darwin. After that he came back and used Mission barge and free labour to get the bullseye mesh out from Truscott and ship it away.

I think might be half money went to himself and half to Mission. Mick was in charge of everything there, the whole operation at Truscott. I only know the stuff went to Darwin. I heard rumours that all that steel went to Japan, don't know if it's true, somebody would've made a bit of money.

Aboriginal people didn't have nothing—all that hard work and no pay! I don't know whether it's true, but people said Mick later owned a motel in Darwin. I heard story like that and that he also bought one in Perth. He had one son too and a wife, Joy Davies and son Michael, they live in Kalumburu and stay there for long time. They live there after all that work finish. Later he went back to Darwin. He lived in the shack at the airstrip; we used to have a yarn when we went walkabout.

When the Truscott work was finished, mission got a truck from there too, old Ford like big army truck with a short body. Mission took the steel board out and you know what, when Vernon Gerard came from Carson River he bought it, don't know how many pound he paid for it. He put the truck on a ship and brought it to Wyndham, where he used it for a while. He wasn't married then. He was living in Wyndham.

The Aboriginal mission labourers all came back empty-handed from that work at Truscott, no money in those days for them. Well, they were used to that.

We root the snakes out with the plough

Before we had the tractor, they first used a horse to pull the plough, a single one. When the tractor came—an Allie* from Truscott, I think—we used that to pull the plough. It was run by power kerosene and we start it with petrol. There were two kind of kerosene in those days; 'home lighting kerosene' for fridge and for lamp, and 'nother one was 'power kerosene', and that was used for the tractor. When the engine runs we shut the petrol off and open the tap for kerosene. One time Brother Ildephonse got accident when he was turning the handle to start it. We had to crank it round and round to start it up. He forgot it was in gear one time and when it start, it took off and he got run over. I'm not sure if he went to hospital for that; his thigh was bandaged after, but he was all right later.

Me and Francis Waina used that little tractor and the plough with the four blades on the side. Francis drove the tractor and I used to control the plough. We used to start ploughing September to October before the Wet comes. We used that paddock opposite the mission where all the mangos are now and Tingun Paddock. That's why I put my name in the bottle tree at Tingun Paddock cause I work there a lot. It's still there today; I saw it. In 1953 I think it was when I did that work. We start to plough that paddock from September and when we finish, the workers come and collect the sticks and roots that the plough pull up; the people collect 'em and clear the paddock.

* Allison Chambers

When we plough the field, the soil goes up and down, plough tip it over and it goes dry within few hours. If there is too many weeds we go over it again. Soil smells very good when it's like that, fresh. Plough could be dangerous too, because when it hit a stump the blades jump up. Brother told us not to put our foot there in that spot, 'You won't have no foot left if you do,' he used to say.

Sometime we root the snakes out with the plough. One day we kill one; we thought it might bite us. Snake stay underneath in the holes they have underground 'cause it's cool there, out of the heat and the sun. It's really good fun to sit there on the plough and watch everything as you go along. We had a waterbag too, good old drinking water it was, better than what we take in the eskies we have now. They hold a lot of water, those bags, I must get one for next time we go in the bush.

Later on when paddock was ready to be seeded, we used to go to the mission and collect bag of peanuts that is already shelled. That was left for ploughing into the ground, they were cleaned by hand and we take it to the paddock. Father Basil tell us not to eat that because they put poison in the bag with the peanuts against the rats, so they won't eat it. It was white stuff, no cockroach or mouse eat it, no idea what it was they put in. We put that in the seeding machine, fill that up and later get urea and put it in 'nother section for fertiliser to go in the ground at the same time. The seeds drop down as you go and the fertiliser does that too. The seeding machine was ordered by Father Basil. It come on the barge in pieces and Brother build it. Brother was a farmer too in New Norcia, he knows all about crops.

Him and Father Basil speak English with each other because he was English and Father Basil is Australian. Father Basil was the only one for a while not Spanish in the mission 'til Brother came. The Spanish people speak mostly Spanish with one another but they also speak mixed with English, too. For us they speak English. The Spanish use both languages.

We start seeding in the morning; I used to sit down there on top at the back and Francis drove the tractor. I used to pour the seeds in the seeding machine and shut the lid. In the corner of the big paddock we stop when we run out and have to go and get 'nother bag. Lunchtime we knock off, sometime other people took over. When they were too busy, there was nobody, we carry on ourselves, Francis and I do it all. It took us three or four days to finish the paddock. Father Basil was very pleased with us at the end of the week.

When the tractor or machine break down, parts had to be ordered from Perth. We had to wait to finish ploughing or seeding. Peanuts had to go in before the rain came.

Sometime we seed at night too, when we need to finish it quick before the Wet. Night-time is cooler too, and the tractor had lights. We just want to get the seeds in before the rain came. We used to have torch on at the back. When rain came, it soaked the ground and the seeds can come out. Paddock was all fenced so nothing go in.

You can smell the soil from long way after the rain and when the sun hit it. Later on you can see the little plants come up and up. Soon we used hoes and clean the weed out all 'e way, all 'e way. Bit later, in the cold weather time, peanuts are ready and we pull 'em out. One bunch has lots o' peanuts right around, a whole heap on the roots; one peanut make about thirty or forty peanuts. When peanut ripe, everybody go there, men and women go, and girls. We all go there in one line, and we pull 'im out, all 'e way, we pull 'em out an' leave 'em there to dry. Then we collect 'em, put 'em in a heap and 'nother heap that way, later on a truck come and we throw it on the truck. After long time mission got a harvester machine—he does everything, and even put 'em in bags.

We had a rope to help the peanuts slide out of the truck when we pull it. Then after we used to pull 'em out and put 'em in a bag or drum. Then we used to clean the leaves and dirt from the nuts. We used to stand up and pour the nuts from a bucket to the ground, let it fall and the wind blow leaves and dust and dirt away. Peanuts were stored in drums with holes in the bottom, to give 'em air, and the drums stand on top of some timber. People could eat peanuts every day. People roast 'em or eat 'em raw, they're good to eat like that too. They get dry and hard. Salted peanuts not as good as that, they make you thirsty for water. We like peanuts. We grew up with peanuts. Afternoon tea time, people used to get peanuts out of a fruit tin. They used to be nice and fresh.

We used to plant sorghum, too, at the same time, in 'nother paddock opposite the windmill, where the big bamboo is now, where the Laoar Creek swings around. That's where sorghum bin grow. That small plough was used for the sorghum field, too. Now there are trees grown there. For sorghum too, we used to make the seeder opening smaller. Sorghum was used to feed the pigs and the chickens. I used to boil the sorghum at night and feed it to the pigs in the morning.

When sorghum gets very high, we used to cut them with the sickle in the dry season, we didn't have no cane knife then. They are very large and are used to cut sugar cane. We used to walk along and cut the sorghum by hand with a short sickle. Many people were needed to do that. We just leave it lying there. Others come along with the secateurs and cut the sorghum heads off with secateurs and put 'em in a bag, and the Chev truck come and load it up. Then, after, we used it for feeding chooks and pigs. In Africa they used it for flour, that's what Brother told us, they don't waste nothing there. I used to boil the sorghum for the pigs and feed it to them in the morning. I feed the pigs with the slops each day—by gee, I used to be smelly and messy and dirty all 'e time I used to go there with the wheelbarrow. I had a shower straight after.

The green stuff, the sorghum leaves and stalks we leave it there and when it's dry we put a match and burn it. Later, mission had a sorghum harvester. Machine sorted it and put it in hessian bags. I used to grab the bags and lift 'em up and throw 'em on the truck. Sorghum seeds didn't get any poison on it; we had enough of it. Mission didn't worry about the rats because they couldn't finish the sorghum if they wanted to, there was heaps there.

I did mostly good jobs there in the mission, all farm work. Francis and me, we did good work there, we had a good time together, we didn't argue or anything. We used to share work and love doing the work, grease all the plough and the tractor. Father Basil gave us a T-shirt and singlet for doing good work. There was no money those days, money would have bin better, but we didn't get any. When I was younger, I could load all the heavy bags, and

Francis used to stack 'em. We used to chat sometime and we work well together. He is like cousin to me. Francis used to work in the garage a lot, but I did mostly farm work.

Sometime I was at the garage for loading, but it was enough I knew about farm work. People didn't have a choice what work they do, when the job come up you do it. Father make work program and Brother used to tell everybody what to do. Everybody was willing in those days. Now and then machine break down, something lose or jammed, and it had to be fixed. We checked it for oil and fuel, every second day we grease it up. We didn't know about other mechanical things. Later on the new plough came, Father Basil ordered new, big plough and it came by boat, and the little tractor pull the new plough all the way from Longhani landing.

When I went to Tingun Paddock lately, I find the old plough there; they just left the plough standing next to the paddock under a big old boab tree. It bin standing there for a long, long time and all the red colour it had before is gone now. They should have taken it to the mission so people can see it when they visit.

Mission store

For long time people never seen money in mission. Only in the 1960s, people were given money by the mission from the pension that they get from government. Pension went straight to mission and mission used to sort it out how much people could get. What that means is that mission had a book like an account book for pensioners.

There was no shop in the community like now, only the monastery had a store. Mission brought everything out on a table on Saturday once a week. The food and things was kept inside the monastery, but on Saturday afternoon they have to bring a table out and put the things on. People could get what they want, they could buy flour, tea and sugar, clothes, ice cream and cool drinks—me and Brother used to bring it out to the table just in front of the monastery.

People, who were paid cash then for work, after a while, had some money and paid straight. Pensioners didn't know what money was and they didn't know how much the government paid them. It came through community welfare. When they get items from the store, Brother used to write it down in the book. Even if they did know what money they had, they wouldn't understand about money. They were only interested in getting tea, flour, sugar, biscuits and tobacco, that's all. Pensioners wouldn't know how much they had left in their account after they buy things.

Flour, tea and sugar used to be free before, but in the '60s, mission didn't give 'em free any more. Money used to come from government to mission for pensioners. From mission, it was supposed to go to the people for few things they want to get from the mission. But mission kept it for pensioners.

Some money did go outside too, 'cause mission used to order things for the people. They used to deal with Boans Store in Perth. Boans sent a catalogue and people pick which thing they want from the pictures. What bin ordered came by plane, like radiogram, or radio, anything like that they used to order in Perth.

Some people used to save money too (£1 used to be a lot). They saved it in the mission. Mission was like a bank, like they do now, these days. Brother used to be in charge of it. People go and give it to the Brother and he put 'em in the envelope with name on it. People save any time they want, like now. If they want to withdraw it, they could. Mission keep a book and people got docket how much they had in the mission, so they knew. That's the people that could read. They never seen a bank book there, they didn't know what bank was. The only person who see a bank was me, when I went away to Kununurra; there I saw what bank account was, that was in the '60s.

Some of this happens still today—some old pensioners never see their money. It goes straight to the community store instead of the mission.

observations of
a Kwini man

What happened to our dances?

Now, today, I'm going to talk about dances, different dances what I remember when I was a boy. They used to dance *pulga*, that's the name of one dance. It was danced by Kulari people, that pulga and *juluroo*, two different dances. Juluroo they used to dance after the war in Kalumburu, next to the big bottle tree still standing there today, in the open where the cemetery is, where the old road to the airstrip went out. The road followed all along past the old cottages, where the people lived.

They built a kind of lean-to there, they used to call that *woorro*, made like the roof of a bough shed. That's a shed with only a roof on but no walls, mainly just for shade. It was used as a screen and the dancers come out from behind it. So sometime in the night we used to go up there to watch, when I was a boy in the mission dormitory.

This is how the songs were made: people go out in the bush and when they stay out that's how they find things and form songs. They make songs about the river or about mountains or animals, or people, how they hunt or fish, or sometime they make songs about devils or spirits or *jilinga*. Jilinga was a bush woman you know. People just go walkabout and think, or sometimes, dream about making songs and dances. They may be resting or sitting down. They might be one or two people make up a song, husband and wife might be, like that old song *jorrmulla* that was done by that old Alec; they used to dance that in Kalumburu, too. Jorrmulla is 'nother dance belong to old Alec, and Kulari and Kwini people could dance it. Jorrmulla is a Kulari dance. Oh, that one they used to dance with *pulmurra* too, they made drawings of fish on wooden boards (pulmurra) that were used in the dance. Kwini people dance only their own dances but the Kulari people dance their own and Kwini dance, too. When men were hunting they make one form of dance; or when they need rain they sing and dance to make rain come.

Only older people make songs and dances for corroboree. Young men do the dances too, but they don't form the songs or the dances, because only the old people got in their mind what bin happen before. Can't make one song straight away, you need to join what's happened together with the other. When you make corroboree, it's got to be like a string, a long line: that's how people form what comes into a story and the story comes with the land itself. From the story comes the song and then the dances are made for the song. You can't separate the song and dance from the land: they all go together.

People make the rule how to do it and who will do the dance. Later some young people dance with them too. They like to join sometime. That's how they learn. Basil (Kulari Elder, Kalumburu) made 'nother pulga dance. Before that it was Augustin that made 'nother joonba dance. Now it's only Basil left who makes them. Pulga songs are part of the corroboree and joonba too. Corroboree is one big thing. Songs that go with it can be joonba or pulga. Corroboree is for show; only thing, you need to find out which songs they have. Joonba, pulga or *wungga*. Wungga song people sing with didgeridoo and clapsticks to mark the rhythm.

Different tribes make different songs and dances. With pulga dance you can tell the difference because people hold the pulmurra when they dance. They are decorations that people hold up behind their head or in their hands, that's pulga. Joonba dance is different again: people when they dance wear tree leaves around their knees, and they wear a hat made out of paper bark, shaped like an ice cream cone, and long beards. The beards were made out of tree bark from the *ulan* tree. They used to get the clean bark on the inside and smash it to make it come up like soft wool, like fibre. That's what they used as a beard. We also used to dip some of that soft bark into honey, when it was collected in a *wanda* (bowl) and take the bark out and suck the honey off it. The paperbark hats were very long and high; they tie it with a string round and round. They also wear paint, whatever they can find, red ochre and white bush paint, too. Sometime they dance with sticks but no pulmurra. You can hear the difference between songs by the sound because words are different, language go with the dance. Pulga songs are sung in Kulari language, like Basil's own songs and dances. Pulga is different to joonba dance because that joonba is Kwini dance.

Wungga dance is with the didgeridoo, the other dances have clapsticks, but wungga has clapsticks and didjeridoo as well, might be it come from top end, Port Keats, or further that way. Only all the men dance together, the young boys slowly join in when the old ones dance, that's how they learn. The parents teach them. The girls and women only dance wungga. Women only dance one side following the men, but they don't play didgeridoo. Sometime women dance their own secret dance where men are not allowed to look.

Yirumi is 'nother dance. Mostly Kwini dance it during the war, sometime Kulari dance it too. People decorate themselves differently for this dance, they hold leaves and twigs in their hands when they dance, nothing else.

The songs and dances travelled around. When one's finished singing the other one would start. When the time was through they take it somewhere else, to Forrest River or Wyndham, leave it in the Overflow, where all the old pensioners live long time ago. They call it the Overflow because they live along the water, the old people. Welfare used to look after them with rations. Lot of Mirriwung people know about pulga, people used to dance pulga too at the Overflow. Kununurra wasn't built yet then. Our people take it to Mirriwung people and they used to take it somewhere else as far as Twelve Mile, leave it there and then the people come back to Kalumburu.

Kulari used to take the dances as far as Mowanjum, near Derby. People and their songs and dances used to move about without the vehicle a long way in those days.

When I started to live in the mission as a child, people dance nearly every day of the week. We didn't always go and see them. When people are sick or die or at burial time, nobody don't dance, 'til a while after, then people sing again. Sometime we used to ask Brother if we can go see the dances. He said, 'I'll ask Father if we can go to see the dance tonight after tea.' Nuns bring all the girls too. They dance near the old cottages. There used to be clear place under that big mango tree, all that was dancing area, it was no mango then in those days. Mango tree came after. There was a shady parkinsonia tree in that place, as big as the mango tree it was, pretty big, nothing there now, the Agricultural Department must have bin poison them all. That was dancing area that, lots of old people danced in those days, a lot of old people. Even when the kids were in the dormitory, they could still be taught dances by their parents. I'm the only one never dance because I was too shy. No one tell me how to do it.

The songs and the dances make corroborees. Mission didn't like certain corroborees and that 'nother dance, that *kurranganda*. Certain people danced that out in the bush where nobody knows. It was a sacred dance.

Once we children found some kurranganda boards in a cave, we found it and left them. Father Cubero was with us and he said, 'We'll pick them up on the way back'. They were flat boards with a white stripe painted on it, about ten or twelve, round, and on sticks, pattern only one stripe. Kwini people saw the smoke of our fire and came and collect them and hide them. When we returned to pick them up, only one small one was left and we took it to the monastery. I think they kept it in the library.

I do remember one time they burn kurranganda boards in the mission compound. You know where the church is facing, there used to be a gate on the road to the Kwini camp. On mission ground, between the church and that museum, out in the open where everyone could see, Father Sanz burn the sacred boards. I don't know where they came from or who brought them in, but they put kerosene on it. One Brother and Father Sanz did that. I saw him. A lot of people were there standing around, Kwini and Kulari people. I don't know how many sticks there were, I don't know who brought them there. The people all went off to the bush after that, that's all I remember, maybe Laurie Waina might know. I didn't know what boards they were, but people told me a long time after, and they were upset. That happened long before we found the other kurranganda boards. Kurranganda dances became less over time, mostly it bin wiped out.

Now I say people these days don't dance because everything is lost. From the beginning, people were dancing all the time, culture was full, that means full of things like our language, our way of life, our *Lalai* (Dreamtime).

They never dance joolooroo, kurranganda, jorrmulla, yirrami and joonba any more because the old people all passed away. With the young generation, everything is lost. They speak English and know very little or nothing of our language. Everything was changed because of the mission policy. We lost everything; once it is lost, we cannot find it again, or we can find only little bit.

Whether some people can redo what has gone now, that I don't know. There are two ways we look at what happened: when nobody was there, no white people, everything is in one piece, but when the kartiya (white people) came, well, lot of things fall apart, little by little. I was away too, working on stations when I was in my twenties. I wasn't there to teach others. Besides, I wouldn't have known what to teach, I didn't know myself, I didn't get to it in the first place.

Aboriginal painting shouldn't have white man name

There is a lot of rock art in my country at Oomarri and in other places in North Kimberley. In West Kimberley, there are mostly Wanjina paintings. They're different. Further north there are others and they are Kwini paintings. Ngarinyin people nowadays call 'em Guyon paintings. White people think they're called Bradshaw paintings, but I'll tell you how that is really wrong altogether.

In Kalumburu, when I was in the dormitory, I discover some near what they call shooting range. We did a lot of walking, but we boys didn't see any. We used to look for wild bush plum in the rainy season, that's how I found the painting. We only noticed that one, because that was our stopping area. I was very young then, we were here and there rock climbing and swimming, but we never saw any others. Maybe we took no notice at that time. Later I found many others there.

But in Oomarri area there are lots both side of the gorge. Wherever I went I seen paintings. I'm really sure it is Kwini painting. My people used to stay there, come through there on the way to the sea. That my birthplace, near the water and I knew from the start that was my own people's painting. The old people told me all the time I was born along that river. They didn't mention the painting. Nobody mention the paintings those days, the old people don't talk about it, but maybe they might've thought don't go near it, because that's where the people were. Their spirits are there now. You can feel it when you're there. The painting is still there, no matter how old it is, when the paint nearly worn out, or change colour, you know they're old. You know that people had been there before, you look at the rocks there; people might have been sitting on it.

Some paintings, you have to lie down to look at it. The older paintings is proper on top where you can see, some worn out by the sun at the edge of the cliff. All paintings are under rocky over hangs; they're protected from the weather that way a bit. Our tribe has bin there, they paint in certain places where they thought the painting has to be. People has bin stand up on the rock to do the painting. Not far, I saw campsites, too, where I find stone spear-heads and tools. In lots of places among the rocks, I can see old fire place near the painting. That's where people chip the stone to make spear and axe; I found some.

I didn't see the paintings when I was small, I don't remember. I must have bin see some paintings, but I don't remember. When I went back, I feel very much that I was just coming back there; coming to the place I was born, where I belong really.

This time when I live in my birthplace, I think a lot. My people has bin there and I have bin there, when I was young. I feel two things, sadness and happiness. When I saw the painting in some part I feel happy inside, some other part you feel a bit sad because you not bin there for long time. When I was small I walk around with my parents. Now I feel reminded that all my people were around me long time ago—that make me happy.

Sad part is that my people have passed away and I was taken to the mission. I was told my mother passed away some-where and nobody could look after me. Once my people lived at Oomarri and travelled through there. The place is so isolated, very tough country, my country. But people lived here, nothing to disturb them. They must 'ave bin happy. They had a lot of knowledge about painting, they didn't have pen or paper or anything to write on, they used their own paint that they made and they painted beautiful pictures on rock that last much longer than any paper. I heard, some people think the paintings are 18,0000 years old or more.

Make me feel good that my people live there long time. I feel good there when I see the painting 'cause Oomarri is one place where very few white people go, so everything there remind me of my own people and how there was many of them round that place. We were a large tribe once. I don't see much of my own people now, only when I'm in Kalumburu, and there's not too many left anyway. The rest of the place where I go, in towns and in the city, mostly I see no sign of my people. Place is full of white people and people from other countries, and sometime I don't see a single one Aboriginal person anywhere. That's why, when I'm in Oomarri, I feel at home really, everything there reminds me of my people, specially the painting.

Nobody showed them where to paint. Only when they saw the place they choose a spot to paint, safe places, nothing can destroy it. To get there is not that easy, they're not on level ground much. At painting sites, I look if they left anything behind on the ground, like red ochre or anything they done with their hands. We found a few, and there are camping areas among the rock too. In the rainy season they could find shelter under the rocks.

Might be my people left those paintings for next generation to look at and remind them. I think their spirits are still 'round there. If you sleep there by yourself you hear lots of sounds at night, noises among the rock, footsteps of people. It can happen if you stay by yourself, you hear how people walk in the grass too, with breaking branches. Yeah, you can still hear sound of footsteps. Many, many people used to go up and down passing through here all the time, go to the coast; go fishing.

Long time ago, one white man told me Aboriginal paintings was on the lower ground because people were lazy to climb up. That's not right. I discover them mainly higher on the mountains. Some paintings are right at the top, some are at ground level but most are higher up, you have to climb up to it to get there and it's not easy. Sometime we saw just like one painting and sometime it's like a big gallery from end to end.

Paintings show people dressed for dancing or with the spear or boomerang, and *umba* (kangaroo) or *pardao* (bandicoot) and *koyo*, the crocodile. There are people in the paintings, they're like people but they're spirits, *jimi*, good spirits. The way they have bin painted they're like floating, just like people bin float past in the air with their feet point downward. They look like a real people with *ngadarri* (paperbark hats) on their head shaped like a cone. Pieces of string go round and round, sometime you can still see the hair come out or they used mud or wax to make the hair stiff and hard so you could put it in a special *moodooroo* (hairstyle) for dance. You don't hardly see the face in the painting, only the shape, not the eyes or anything. The body is mainly thin and long, very thin, with a bit of a tummy in the front, long legs and long arm, and narrow shoulders. The arms they got *doonggool* (tassles) hanging down, from there to here, both side and the belt they wear is still hanging down, too. They also wear *nyogoo* (hip covers).

They used to smash a tree bark on a rock to make string. It come out all white. Special tree you see it sometime, you smash the bark, make it soft like a brush—that's what we use to tie hair like in the paintings. 'Nother *ngoonooroo* (string) is made of human hair.

Rock paintings have spears, made out of wood, used to spear kangaroo or human being. One end is barbed, like a spear gun, when you spear something it won't come out. A stone spear, when you spear anything, it breaks inside.

The colour in the paint range mostly between brown, orange or mauve colour, mostly it is red, burnt orange colour. I have seen these paintings all the way from Kalumburu to Pago and to the King George River. Paintings are found mostly near water, that's where people hang around. Never bothered to look near Forrest River Settlement for painting 'cause too many people has bin massacred there. Forrest River (now Oombulgurri) is three or four days walk from Kalumburu.

All that kind of painting bin called Bradshaw painting and this is how that is wrong: about 1890 came this Englishman named Bradshaw. He was a surveyor. He travelled through the Kimberley and saw our paintings. He asked Aboriginal people 'bout them but the Aboriginal people told 'im: 'This is not our painting, they're no good'. So he went away and told the white world about the paintings and what the Aboriginal people said, and the paintings were called after him from then on 'til this day.

That name is wrong because they're Aboriginal painting—shouldn't have white man name. Aboriginal people lived there before. They did the painting. White man has no right to give Aboriginal painting white man name. Aboriginal people been here for very long time, our painting been out there and is still there on the rock today.

Like old Mary Pandilo, my cousin sister, old Aunty Mary, said about every bit of the paintings. It's got name in our language she said, 'They're *jimi*, they're here one minute and gone the next,' that's what she said and she knows it all.

Might be that Bradshaw man asked Ngarinyin person, he might 'ave asked the wrong person. Or might be he asked the right person, but it happens that they didn't want him near the paintings and they told him lies to make him go away. As a white man, he didn't know which was the right or the wrong person that belong to the paintings, and no Aboriginal person trust any white man they don't know. I think Aboriginal people didn't want him there, that's why they didn't explain to him what painting it was.

Now, there is this 'nother man living in eastern state. He's Graham Walsh. He is a white man who came and take picture of the rock art all around in the north Kimberley, in my country, too. He says Bradshaw painting not really done by Aboriginals. He believe the paintings are not Aboriginal. He says paintings are too beautiful, too good for Aboriginal people to do them. He's really absolutely wrong. It seems all the white people agree, they don't know any better. My argument is he's very much wrong. I am right because Aboriginal people live here, they did the painting all the time. Old people still alive today, all say this was done by our people.

Graham Walsh took all that big photographs. He didn't ask any permission from our people or myself. He didn't ask anybody whether the painting sites were sacred or spiritual or any other thing, he just took pictures and make 'em into a big book. I see that book myself. Aboriginal Affairs lent it to us. Book is pretty big with photos of the rock art and the name of places where that man been, and he never asked enough questions. He went there without proper and full permission, just like some other people we know.

I seen articles published about the *Bradshaw* paintings and Graham Walsh all over the place in tourist magazines and newspapers, so more and more people believe what he says 'cause they don't know any better. I tried to tell as far as I can go that it is wrong. I said that at the Oral History Conference in Alice Springs in 1997, and the people that were there are informed now what is the right thing.

The old man that passed away in Derby, and others like Ngarinyin Elder Paddy Neowarra from Derby, went to Paris in 1997. They went to the outside world to tell 'em that these *Bradshaw paintings* are really Aboriginal paintings. Well, I think Ngarinyin people went to Paris, but Kwini people didn't go because few left of my tribe and they didn't know about the trip. I didn't get informed and people in Kalumburu never bin told what happen outside, they're too isolated, and maybe they don't care any more. In Derby, information pass easily. I could've went too, if I'd known. I could have went still and all, but I had no idea. The Ngarinyin people call the paintings *Guyon Guyon*. I've heard this before but it's not my language. Guyon Guyon means, "the people from a long time ago". Later, I read about that trip to Paris by chance in a magazine, one year later.

I am not happy about this Graham Walsh. He never asked enough Aboriginal people first, never consulted us properly. People shouldn't take photographs without asking. It is my people's Aboriginal art and we cannot just be ignored, because we are the voice for our people. I talk like that because our voice has to be heard from someone. People should come and consult us. The world must get information from the right people, not the wrong people. We are the right voice and they should talk to us.

There are other people who take pictures of our art and make money. 'Nother white man takes photos of our Guyon Guyon painting and he sells them right in the market. He makes cards out of it. *Made in England*, that's what's printed on them. There's no information on it to say the picture come from WA, or is market. Is only name of the photographer on the cards, not of our people who did the paintings. He's making money from our art without our consent or agreement and there is no law against it in Australia—I tried to find out. I talk about it to a lot of Aboriginal people and no one seems to know how to stop that from happening. There is no law to protect that art.

I'm really concerned that white people set themselves up as expert on Aboriginal rock art. I like 'em to consult Aboriginal people, because all the rock art on this continent, Australia, has bin done by Aboriginal people. They were the only ones living here for very long time.

I like to see people talk to us soon as they look at Aboriginal things, so they find out the right information—that's how it ought to be.

Police patrol

In the Kimberley in those days when not many white people lived there yet, the patrols used to start from Wyndham, which was the only town then in the north-east Kimberley. The old police station is still standing there today. It also used to be the court-house, but now they've turned it into a museum for the tourists. There was no Kununurra then; that came much later.

Police collect people who'd done something against the white law. They also had to get people with venereal disease, lepers and other sick people to take 'em to the hospital in Wyndham or Derby. They put 'em all on the chain; otherwise they'd run away. Chain was the only thing that keep 'em there; they run away because they was afraid of police 'cause of all the killing the police got in their mind. They were especially afraid of the police after what was done in the Forrest River massacre, where the police kill a lot of people there, men, women and children. That was only not very long ago in 1926. People are still remembering it very well today. In 1945, it was only 20 years back.

In the 1940s, when the police came to Kalumburu, I remember one constable Laurie Shaw. He came there a lot of time, not only to Kalumburu, but also to do the round on the stations Kerangie, Gibb River, and Ellenbrae. Kalumburu Mission was a stopping place, and then they go straight to Forrest River Mission and from there, back to Wyndham. Usually the patrol had one policeman and several police boys, I don't know if they had more sometimes, I heard later that they did.

On police patrols, they carried a lot of things. They went on horseback and also took a number of packhorses for carrying supplies, a good number of them; we saw that as they passed through. They carry food, tea, flour, sugar, tobacco, tin food and firearms, mostly .303 and .22 rifles, revolvers and .38 Colt like in the cowboy films. I read in the archive that they always carried several hundred rounds of ammunition an' several bags of chain and handcuffs and locks.

Our people were tied up with the chain round their neck. It was like a heavy iron collar, round, and they were tied one to the other in a line together. While the police was riding horses, their prisoners had to walk behind the horse for hundreds of miles. No road there, only horse tracks in the '40s. Sometime the iron ring round the neck was too tight, and at least one man died because of it. When on the march, the chain that held the prisoners was tied to the horse that carried the police. Sometime horse get in a fright and bolt and run and drag the prisoners. I saw one case recorded in the archive when I was looking in there; there must have bin more like that. One horse got in a fright, it threw the policeman and then it took off dragging prisoners along.

Police came to the Mission one day when I was in the dormitory. It was Constable Brown on a patrol; I think he came twice. John Brown that was his name. We knew him when they came there with two trackers. The police camp in the monastery and the police boys camp near the river somewhere. They eat what they brought; police was fed in the mission. Once police and two police boys went on the mission lugger to Sir Graham Moore Island for a few days fishing and looking for turtle.

After that, two nanny-goats were killed for them, they wanted the meat for the patrol. They cut it up, 'cause I think it was to be salted. Patrols stay in the mission for a week mostly so that the horses could have a rest. Horses need a rest from working. Sometime they get poor from walking and carrying loads, too. On stations and missions, the patrol stay for one or two weeks so they can have a good rest. From Kalumburu Mission, they go straight to Forrest River Mission, and from there, right around to the Pentecost River Crossing, and on around to Wyndham on the old road. Then they pass through the pumping station and across the marsh, and then there's Wyndham town on the Cambridge Gulf.

In the archive, when I look at the government records, I find out that sometime police from the Pilbara even went across to the Fitzroy River to kidnap Aboriginal people for work as pearl-divers or for pastoral stations. Pilbara is a long way from the Kimberley. S'ppose they think they make it harder for the Kimberley people to get back home. Maybe they thought they won't find their way back, but Aborigines always find a way where white people cannot. That kidnapping is another reason why Kimberley people are frightened of police.

Police also did chain women on those patrols whether they were sick or not. I read in the police report in the archive the police sergeant even checked women for venereal disease right there in the bush. I don't know how they could do such a thing! That's not proper for a man to do, only a doctor can, and they wasn't a doctor. I don't think Aboriginal men would do that. I feel really sorry for these women that they had to put up with it. I think these diseases were brought in from somewhere—we didn't have the new diseases the white people brought to us, and the women must've felt real bad.

Sometime, when they were in a chain, a few people managed to escape. Must be with help from one of the police boys. It was good for my people but no good for the police because I think they were paid meal allowance for prisoners, and I think that might've bin hard if they had lost all the prisoners on the way. Well, in the archive I find out that some prisoners complain that they didn't get fed some days at all.

While I live in the mission I never see any prisoners in chains in Kalumburu—I'm not sure why, 'cause we saw the police and the trackers all the time. I did know that Aboriginal people has bin chained and taken through the bush for as far as they could walk. I was told by older people, several times over the years. They never really said much about it—you couldn't do nothing when you're afraid of white people who have guns and our people had nothing.

I heard 'nother story that some old people in the camp tell me when they came to the mission: that the police used to kill people's dogs. The old people were really sad about it. They said police kill our dogs and they were frightened of the police because of that, too. I still thought they only shot the sick dogs perhaps, but I see they shot all the dogs all the time wherever they go. I was finding out more about that in the archives. It seems the police must a bin getting paid scalp money for the dogs; they took the scalps, see. Now in the records I notice they really did collect the scalps and some of the mission people complained to the police about it. I think a scalp was worth a few shilling.

In some cases, they didn't shoot 'em—they kill the dogs with a tomahawk, right in front of the owners. I don't know why the dogs didn't run away, might be they tied 'em up. Dog can bite too if they come closer, they must a bin tied 'em up, they didn't like to waste a bullet. That is so cruel. Some people got very upset to see their dogs killed just like that, they run off and never come out of the bush again. That was such a bad thing to do. A dog is most important part of Aboriginal life; dog save people's life, they give warning of danger, and they hunt all the time. That's why people keep dogs, especially old people who can't hunt any more. Dogs do it for them; they kill goanna and small animals like that because the dogs can get 'em, so the old people can eat.

Around that time somebody from the police went all over the Kimberley and report they only saw old people and the sick. He don't realise young ones went away so police can't catch 'em. The people that could walk well all run away, so he thought only old and sick are left.

When I was a child we didn't think about police boys doing that work with white police. We accept everything. Now I know that once Forrest River Mission sent a man to be police boy to Wyndham, just because they think he's a troublemaker in the mission. It look like he was sent to Wyndham because police were looking for 'nother police boy at that time. I don't think anyone ask if he want to go.

I also know that police boys, as they were working, some time escaped later. Some turn against the police like Pigeon of the Bunuba tribe in the Kimberley. He did it the tough way, he learned shooting and other thing from the police as a tracker and police

*Ambrose (back row next to Fr Isadore) and children—Kalumburu Mission,
late 40s to early 50s*

Traudl

Guyon Guyon rock paintings at Oomarri, Ambrose's place of birth

View from the top of high rock formations, Oomarri

Traudl

Another of the Guyon Guyon rock paintings, Oomarri

Church service with L to R: Fr Wilfred, Abbot Rt Rev. Gregory Gomez, Fr Maur Enjuanes, Ambrose Chalarimeri and Francis Waina as altar boys. The interior and the formal context illustrates a sharp contrast of spiritual traditions related to the land

boy, and then he turn against 'em to help his people. Jandamarra, that his proper name, we all know about him. Only later when I'm older I read his story in a book. He was pretty good for helping his own people. He shot one policeman. His grave is still there in Derby. He did that because they are his own people he captured; that's why he turn around to help them. That's the same way as some of our police boys did, like one fella called Damper—when the white police wasn't there, he let the prisoners free and then escape with them one time.

Well, the police tracker, they were there only to help police catch who ever they went for, lepers, or other people they were after, you know. They can tell by the tracks where they went and go to the place where they camp. Their job is to find a way to go to the stations and all the places on a patrol where police need to go. There was no road and the white people didn't know the bush. I don't think police boy was allowed to use firearms or take prisoners; only the police was s'pposed to do that.

From the reports I saw it was only one policeman going on patrol mostly and all the rest were police boys. No other white person to keep an eye on him, so he could do what he likes. If there were two or three, it could've bin different. He was the only one to write a report and he can put anything in it, no one to check or investigate what it was.

Aboriginal people suffered a lot, and where could they go and complain against white people? No one would believe Aboriginal people anyway, not even today.

I know that sometime things went wrong in a very bad way on the police patrol, especially for my people. Once in 1944, somebody went on patrol to Cape Voltaire region. In the map, you can see it's a land point near where the Mitchell River flows into the sea. Police supposed to capture several people who bin in tribal fighting. There were three police boys, one sergeant and two Aboriginal women seem to belong to the trackers; one of them was the horse tailer.

They captured some people, but others was still missing, so they made a camp and the police sergeant send two trackers to look for more people. As they went a long way walking they found a track in a beach. When they saw Aboriginal people was on an island just there, this police boy made a fire on the shore to attract the people on the island. When they saw the smoke, the people on the island get in a canoe and come to see, but soon as they notice it was the police, they realise there was a big danger for them. They turn around quick to get back to the island, but the police boys fire at them immediately.

One man in the boat was killed and one was wounded. People in the canoe got very much frightened and think safest way was to go to the mainland and then they were captured. From there, one tracker went back to the camp where the police sergeant was and the other prisoners. He told 'em what happened and when the police heard the story about one bin killed and one wounded, he himself walk down there—took 'im long way. He left the other prisoners there in the camp on the chain, bin look after by one tracker left behind, and the two women.

He walked back long way with one tracker to that beach and when he reached the shore, he took the gun off the police boys. While they were there, the sergeant suddenly saw the smoke, big, black smoke rise in the distance where he thought his camp was near. When the police saw the fire, he knew there was trouble and he walked back long way. In his report he said later he reached there in the morning. Nothing left of his camp. The prisoners were gone. They cut the chains, took all the food. What was left, saddles, bags, swags, everything else, they bin put it in one big heap and burned the lot.

Leprosy—we had no word for it

Many Aboriginal people got infected with leprosy in the northern part of the Kimberley. Around Kalumburu, it seem to come mostly from the coast along Kingana. Many people work for a pearler called Willie Reid there, and that's a place where most visitors come from outside on boats. Kingana is a place out between Truscott and Prince Regent area, somewhere in the middle. Used to be lot of settlements there, Port George and others.

I think leprosy might've come with those Maccassans from Indonesia. Nobody had it before in the bush when I was small, as far as I know. First heard about it when I was about ten and still in the dormitory, old enough that I understand a few things. People didn't call it anything; there's no word for that, cause we didn't have it.

In the mission, I heard doctor was coming around on a routine visit. He found a few people from the bush or the mission with leprosy. I didn't know what the sickness look like. Oh, when I was old enough they explain what it was—only later on in the 1950s and '60s when doctor came and took a few people away to hospital, I saw it. The skin colour look like red and sometime the fingers get sick.

In the early mission days, police went in the bush to round 'em up. When police come looking for criminals on a trip, they were instructed same time to look for people who had leprosy. There were no roads or even tracks for them to go on in those days, all the way from Wyndham to Kalumburu. Police could only go on horseback and with police trackers. Aboriginal trackers know where to go; they know how to find food. White people couldn't go alone. These trips took long time and they had to carry all their gear and supplies. Only in the dry season they could go and come back.

People knew police was the one to get 'em because they were the only ones who live in the bush. People didn't know what exactly police came for, but they thought they might be taken away. They wanted to be in the bush all the time. They were frightened of the police and the chain. They didn't know what was going to happen. So people took off to the mountain mainly, soon as they heard police come. They were frightened the police might do something to them, take 'em away from home, put 'em somewhere else. Well, they frightened to get caught.

Police always catch our people. Some time look for person that might've killed someone. Well, Aboriginal people wasn't really criminal. White people have the most criminals. Aboriginal people only kill for good reason with the spear, as far as Aboriginal law was in those days. They act according to tribal law, like when one man stole 'nother man's woman; he was entitled to kill that one. The white people didn't look at our law properly; they only carry on the white rules. They don't know our laws at all. Old law was good but the kartiya came and put their law over ours, just like they wiped it off and thought their law is better. That's absolutely no good, 'cause our law was all right for us.

Even though police sometime just want to get the sick people to a hospital, Aboriginal people had a good idea what they see and what they going to get. Some they didn't get 'em. People climb up in the mountain 'cause horse can't climb, but horse is faster on the flat ground, so they got some and put 'em in the chain. People knew police always catch Aborigines and tie 'em up in a tree, even the sick people with leprosy. Trouble was police was white and our people even didn't like to see white people, not even ordinary white people, gold miners or station people—they afraid of kartiya, 'cause in those days the white people always kill 'em, specially the police.

Some leprosy people might change their mind because Aboriginal tracker tell 'em what it's for; I don't know. The ones caught got taken to the mission in chains and then they bin transported with the lugger right around to Derby Leprosarium. I think they might've kept watch on them on the lugger 'cause they can swim too.

Leprosarium was right outside Derby. We follow the road from the cemetery, follow the marsh right around. The government run it, had manager and hospital and school there, big place, and people were there for months and years. People from Kalumburu were there too, Francis Waina when he was young, and Liduvina when she was small, Placid, her brother had leprosy, an' Benedict father had it, Ildephonse, and Benedict when he was small, an' Jackie Lefthand went to leprosarium, too, and his brother Manila, that was his name. Wagan went there too, my brother Augustin went there later, and Eileen Frederick and old Solomon Frederick—wait yet—Ignacia and her husband, Gregory Punji, an' husband brother went, even Peter, (Clement father), all that people was there.

Leprosarium had man quarters, woman quarters, girls dormitory, people of all ages was there. If a woman there give birth, the child not allowed there, like Stanley Nangala, his mother born him in Leprosarium—someone else grow him up outside. Only sick children could stay. The rule is nobody goes there, visitors allowed only on Sundays. We used to go there for visit on Sunday, and you know what, when I live in Old Mowanjum (Aboriginal community), we used to go on foot to get a taxi in town, to save money. I was working in Derby then for Don Archer. Old Mowanjum was further past the airstrip, past the other side. We used to walk, and then we wait there in the reserve for taxi to come in line about ten o'clock. We allowed to go to the leprosarium ten o'clock. We visit and talk, walk around free, I went there lot o' time. Same taxi come in the afternoon an' pick same people up.

Leprosarium closed about 1970s or '80s. Few people run away from there, I remember at least two run away, in the '50s, two men. One got lost at Drysdale River, 'nother one come right through to Kalumburu, old Solomon. Solomon bin send to Leprosarium when he was small. The mission didn't send him back. I think he must've bin all right then. He stayed and got married there to Eileen. The other was Leo, Augustin and Robert's brother, he walk away and never come out anywhere and nobody seen 'im since. Leo just walked away from Solomon at night, and Solomon tried to find him for a while, then he walk straight to mission to tell 'em. A search party set out, but it took Solomon long time to walk to Kalumburu, so the search started much later. People from Kalumburu made a search for Leo, but couldn't find him. The two escaped from the Leprosarium in the dry season. Might be it take 'em a couple of months to travel to Kalumburu. They need time to kill kangaroo and fish and goannas as they go. Leo was lost for good. It seems he might've bin a bit sick and lost his mind. That was in the '60s. If you travel on the Gibb River Road nowadays from Derby to Kalumburu, it's about 690km distance. Drysdale River, where the two men crossed it, is more than half way.

Indonesian fishermen

Indonesian fishermen, when they come here to the Australian water, they are arrested these days and get big fines. Their boats are burned. I don't think this is very good at all. The people in the boats don't come to claim the country like the British did or all those other settlers. They don't do no harm, they only come to do the fishing and go back like their people did before. For thousands of years they bin come round and round, they claim nothing. Their people has bin survive for many years, they do exactly nothing wrong.

They drifted by sails only according to the weather. Where they can get hold of the land, they stop and see the places they can get to, see what they can find. I know they made friends with Aboriginal people. Further down the coast in places like Broome and One Arm Point, all along there, you can see Aboriginal people mixed with them. Macassans used to be all along the coastline, right up to Darwin and between Truscott and Kingana side, downwards to Kunmunya Mission near Prince Regent. We mostly had no problem with them.

Some time they stay in Broome or One Arm Point, that's how some Aboriginal people are related to them, you can see it. When the men landed and stayed, they look for some women now and then. Some of the men took our women. How often that happened, I don't know. They used them for friends and they leave them, they didn't take 'em away, they never do. Around

Kalumburu they mostly were in Pago side, that's how that Tamarind tree was there, and that's why the place is called Tamarindo Beach. Lately the tree got burnt, maybe by lightning. Father Rosendo used to go and visit them when they were on that beach; he knew where they camp. Archaeologist Ian Crawford, bin digging there for Macassan pots.

They should let 'em come in and go back again. By doing that they only mind their own business, they don't take things we need. When they come to take trochus shell to make money, that's well and good, they should be left alone by all rights. Aboriginal people let 'em have that fishing right and they entitled to keep it. Sea cucumber they take too, they did that for long time. You can see along the coastline their ovens and fires bin built up with stones near beaches, you can still see them. Sea cucumbers they cook 'em and salt 'em, trade 'em with other Asian people. That has been recorded. Indonesian people used to salt it and hang it, that way it would keep and not go bad.

We call sea cucumber *boodjelooma*. You and me saw small one, but when I went on lugger, I saw big ones. I got in a fright. I thought it was a snake, but Louis said, 'No, it's just a boodjelooma.' Trochus shell mostly round One Arm Point. I think they came for pearls too. They used to dive themselves, the Indonesians; they didn't force Aboriginal people to do that for them.

Our people built boats too, canoes, only they didn't go far to other countries like some other people we know. We satisfied with what we have and we didn't want to go to far away places, cause we had no relations there. We belong to our country.

Aboriginal people only like to go bit further out to the islands. We have canoe made out of a tree with those big leaves, called *murr* along the river. They used to chop it down, make the canoe while the leaves are still green. Murr tree pretty big like the cypress pine. They shape the canoe with an axe, they leave it in the sun to get dry, then it can float. When it's green, the wood is softer; when it's dry, it get hard. Might be about three or four people fit in. I seen one in Kalumburu, where we swim at that place called Jindi, where the crocodiles are.

Some of the canoes the people made were meant for the sea. They made 'em wider and deeper. They were also made out of wood and people carry big fish and turtle and dugong in it, so the boat had to be strong. They were used for hunting mostly. The sides are thin but the bottom has bin build much thicker. I only saw old people, how they cut the tree and shape it. I was in the dormitory then, about twelve years old. We could go and watch 'em do it. If they don't have canoe, they get wood to build a raft and then put paperbark on top. Paperbark, itself, can float too. Tie it round and round and round with fibre from pandanus leaves. Paperbark can take the weight easy, long as it joined together. It's waterproof. Rain time they used it for humpy, lot of ways people used it.

That was long time ago. They all use dinghies now.

We don't want no war gear here

Near Kalumburu, right at the top of the Kimberley, there's a lot of gear left over from the war, just lying around, polluting the environment, make it look ugly. Two places are specially bad, the old airbase at Truscott and Pago, about 28 km north of Kalumburu. Nobody lives there now.

There's rubbish, like 44-gallon drums, bits of aircraft and vehicles, still left over in Truscott. When we went there from Kalumburu in the 1950s, we see tons of drums dumped in the bush. When the war was over, soldiers went home and everything was just left behind. We see a lot of equipment still there, buildings, dongas, car parts an' drums. They even had a picture theatre there too for the army personnel.

We left after lunch on the lugger and reached there in the afternoon, about three or four o'clock. There were heaps of trucks at Truscott, more than a hundred. We still saw an ambulance car even. It was first time I see Truscott. Father Basil took us for few days holiday, so we could have a look. Lot of trucks we saw, all kind, big trucks, small trucks, jeeps, because there was a road everywhere in Truscott to drive on in the war. It was a big air base, lot of jeeps, small one like land rover, sheep truck, grader, old steam roller, they lie scattered, broken down or with flat tyres, all over the place.

Drums was there, cannot count 'em, thousands, 44-gallon drums; most of them are empty, some are water drums, 'nother one for petrol or diesel, and all sort of a big steel for road building. So much wasted there, heaps all along the coastline, some neatly stacked, all with bungs open. But there were a lot of full ones too, standing in the depot, may be more than a hundred. Fuel was kept in the depot, in a big yard, some were still in good order, but many were half buried; they bury them with a machine in three or four pit they had dug there.

Somehow the mission took a few trucks out of that place, but no fuel as far as I know. Mission didn't have generator then. They had a horse to pull the plough; they had one truck, first truck 20 Cart Weight Ford, the barge and a lugger for the mission work. Later, all the rest was from Truscott. I remember this—from Truscott they brought three trucks to the mission, but besides that, mission took 'nother three trucks. The Abbot of New Norcia sent a telegram to have those trucks sent to New Norcia Mission, so we sent some there on the ship *Dorrigo*, I think.

Don't know if mission paid any money for the trucks, or who paid for the transport to get 'em from Truscott to the two missions. It was a pity mission couldn't use some of that fuel that was wasting at Truscott after the war. There was no electricity in mission then, only tilly lamp. They could've used the petrol for the truck and the barge. The tractor was run by power kerosene, it was old model. We used to take it for ploughing the paddocks. Fridge was a kerosene fridge those days, and generator came later. Lot of drums was left over, a good few had petrol in 'em still. I was very surprised to see so much equipment just left there and go to waste.

These days, things might be changed at Truscott, because the army moved back in again later, and has people living there all the time, army personnel. The airstrip was rebuild. They might 'ave cleaned up.

Pago is the place where Kalumburu Mission started in 1908. Mission moved to Kalumburu in 1935. In the war, the defence force used to land many hundred of fuel drums at Pago 'cause Pago coast has deep water. Mission wasn't there any more by then. Drums get there by barge. Fuel was put to shore there to use for machines to help construct the Kalumburu airstrip. Somebody mention there was radio base at Pago.

Army widen the road from Pago to Canbejuat (a jump-up in the hills on the way to Kalumburu). Before, it was a track, made by our people for donkey and cart. Later the army build that road again with a machine during the war. The airstrip in Kalumburu was build by defence force after the war had started. They might 'ave thought they need it for the air force. There bin no other airstrip near there at the time. Mission got bombed in that war by Japanese and people lose their life 'cause that airstrip was put too close to our settlement and mission.

I think the army should get the drums removed now. Should've done it ages ago. Now you see 'em everywhere around the bush at Pago, piles and piles of them, all brown with rust, they look bad, they don't belong in our beautiful bush—they really spoil it. Remind me of war and bombs and bad times. I don't like to walk bare foot on the beach there 'cause it got all the rust there and bits of drums half buried and broken up in sharp pieces. Some are buried in the sand; you can't even walk there any more. One time it was very good, not now.

Pago was a beautiful place, but with all that left over that make it no good, see. Also, some people are making their homeland there at Pago lately. They want to live there outside Kalumburu with their family and they shouldn't have any of that rubbish there. The army used that land for their war machinery and they should've cleaned it up straight after.

A good reason
to complain

In the years I was in the dormitory, all mail, in and
out, was handled in the mission by the Fathers and
Brothers. At that time letters used to be opened. We
children knew that already, but problem has bin find out when one
old man complained about the mission in a letter. It was about the
money line, because he was the only one who had money coming
to him then. He bin living outside for a while, he was a special case.
He knew about the money. He's bin living in Port Hedland for a
while. He had a bank account an' all. We didn't know such things
existed even. He had a good reason to complain about the mission.
Reason was, he wasn't happy the way it was handled. I don't know
exactly what it was the mission did that he didn't like. It was
money for himself, his own money; he was on a pension. In the
end he send a letter one day to Wyndham or Derby Welfare. Laurie
Waina did it for him. He couldn't do it himself, his boys were too
small then to read and write, so Laurie did it for him. He took it to
the mission. He supposed to wait for Brother to take the letter.
Laurie gave it to old man and old man went there and instead of
waiting for Brother to come, the old man left it there, put the letter
on the table and went away.

There was no other way, mission was the one that received
and sent all the mail. People brought their letters to the mission
without envelope—they didn't have any. Brother said, 'All right, I
send it for you.' He used to put it in an envelope later and send it.

Letters were all read even before that old man complained 'bout his money. I know 'cause we seen it. One night when Brother came in the dormitory to lock the door for us, so we couldn't get out, some one in the dormitory—I think my brother-in-law—gave him a letter to post to Wyndham.

We say prayers and Brother lock the door. Soon as he locked the door, he went to the office from there. You know how we caught him? We saw him with the light on in the middle room in the monastery. He put that light on and took the letter and read it. We see it clear at night-time, all the boys was watching him. We had the light off and he had the light on, and we watch. We were getting to know a few things and we say, 'Now what is he going to do?' We know is the same one letter he read, nothing else, it was that letter, we can see.

That 'nother letter from the old man later, Brother read it. Then Father Sanz come and ask people who did the letter for old Charlie? Laurie Waina said, 'I did it.' Father Sanz argue with Laurie He said, 'Why you done that, Laurie?' Laurie said, 'No, that's his words, I did it for him. They're not my words.'

Later, when I left the mission altogether to work outside, Father Sanz told me: every letter that goes out, it's got to be read. We knew that for long time. We knew people's mail bin opened and read. Only one letter that I know about wasn't opened. I was there when it came. That was a letter the Abbot himself sent to Laurie Waina. When they saw the Abbot bin send it, not even the Father or Brother open it. Laurie got it himself. I was there and Laurie told me himself, 'Nobody opened it.'

The Abbot even sent a present for him one day, a camera, 'cause Laurie took photos of the mission. He sent the photos to New Norcia before; he had a little camera himself. Abbot gave him a better one later for present.

When I work outside I used to send letter from the station to my sister Magdalene and my brother-in-law, but when they get my letter to them, it used to be opened. My brother-in-law didn't say anything. People were scared to complain. They know somebody would carry it to the mission. They wouldn't even complain among themselves, they just keep quiet. Somebody would report them. They don't stick together, and people would be told off by mission.

People were frightened to send a letter out after a while, so each time I went back for visits to Kalumburu later, when I work outside, I always take people's letters with me. They didn't want the mission to read 'em, so they gave it to me to post properly this time. People used to tell me things and say, 'Don't tell anyone.' I used to say, 'I won't breathe a word.' There were certain people we all know who would run to the mission and tell. Yeah, they think they do the right thing but they don't realise is their own people they talk about and really they betray them. They didn't think of that.

When they send me letter from Kalumburu, you can't tell if the mission read it first 'cause they the one who post it. On the station, I used to meet the mail plane and I give the mailbag to the missus. The missus sing out to me after, 'There's a letter for you Ambrose!' and she gave it to me unopened.

White men—
Aboriginal women

Long time ago to this day, white men have sex with
Aboriginal women everywhere. I think that wherever you go, you see that. I've seen it myself. We don't
know much about birth control. Women in the communities
mostly don't use any, at least in my days and I think most white
men don't either.

Woman then get pregnant and have a child and child is born a
bright colour. Sometime the men go for a ride with the woman in
a car. They can have sex anywhere they please. They don't go near
the house when the man has a wife. If he's single, they take 'em to
their home. When they got wife, they mostly go out in the bush or
near the river. I have seen it happen. I bin with a few people who
go with white men. When the women get children from them, the
men don't even bother. They don't like to hear about it.

When Aboriginal people go from place to place, there's nothing to worry them; they just stay with community people, they're
welcome any time. But white people don't do that, because white
people cannot go to other white people's house and knock on the
door, unless they're friends, you know. Some white men go to the
communities and have different idea about going there. They come
and want to live there free; they usually end up getting free accommodation, free food, and free sex. Mostly they bring in grog and
drugs. I find out some are criminals and hide from the law. The
more remote the community the better for them. They almost

never do any work; they just sit around all day and every day. They can easily do that in remote, isolated communities. They come to the community and are very friendly to the people. They smile and talk and laugh, so people think they're good men. They mostly have some vehicle to get around in. Sometime they come with food and drink first, ask the people if they want drink. That's how it starts; and then bit by bit, some women go to white people all the time, for sex, money and grog. Some of our men and boys join 'em, too, for grog and drugs, and get hooked. Aboriginal people in the isolated communities sometime just can't tell a good white man from a bad one. That's how women choose the wrong ones, they can't tell the difference. Things go on and on from there, long as the white men come with the drink. I've seen it happen. Only white men do that, not white women.

That's worse in isolated communities but it happens in towns too. White strangers do ask Aboriginal people if they can stay the night. I've seen 'em come. Not in the reserve days, they weren't allowed into the reserve by law unless they see the Welfare first, but that's long ago. Anyone can go there now.

In town when girls wait for lift or taxi or ask men for lift back home, men take 'em to the camp and leave 'em there. If they wanted they could have sex on the way, that's why the men shout the girls in the pub. When the girls get drink all the time, that's when they tell 'em, 'Take me for a drive somewhere.' In a small town, the girls go anywhere to drink, because many love drink. Even I used to shout girls drink just to have sex, that's what everybody got in their mind. Some say no, some say yes, but I never have sex with girls when they're drunk, they might say later I rape 'em. I always beware they might complain. If the girls knock me back, I say, 'That's all right.' A lot of time I got knocked back, but some girls did like me and have a drink with me.

In Kalumburu, they had no mixed children for long time; no white men allowed by the mission to come and go as they do now. There were only the priests and nuns and sometimes army or government men stay for while, but not any of them got girls pregnant in Kalumburu, not that I know of. That word pregnant, well, we never heard that much. Pregnant is very new word for us. We call it the "family way".

Only after the girls left Kalumburu, that's when they got in the family way. We know it didn't happen in Kalumburu, only when they come to town back in '70s, they did that. We did have two cases in Kalumburu of children with white fathers, but they came from outside. One woman brought two half-caste children with her to Kalumburu from Wyndham in 1950s, but that was arranged by the mission. And then we had Willy Reid's children. He was a part Aboriginal from 'nother place. He worked at Kingana, near Kalumburu and his children were Josephine and Eileen. There was no mixed kids other than those four.

All the people married there in the mission and stayed in Kalumburu. They married their own people inside, lots of really wrong marriages. People married their first cousins—happened a lot—even my brother married wrong side, too. Before, they never bin allowed by mission to go outside Kalumburu and we also had no money to go. Only one woman left Kalumburu to live in Broome in the 1960s, but I think she had a special reason. In Oombulgurri, which used to be Forrest River Mission 'til the '60s, it used to be same. When it was a mission, girls couldn't go out. They stayed in the dormitory. When mission left, lot of people went to Wyndham and lots of girls, heaps of them, got pregnant there to white men. None of the white men, who got girls pregnant, married them. They all had wives already.

Around 1982, independence from the mission came for the Kalumburu community. People started to go out into Wyndham and other towns to see the outside world. The women got pregnant to white men there. Before, people only allowed out for medical treatment. Welfare put 'em back on the plane to Kalumburu after seeing doctor. Welfare controlled that with mission. I was away that time when the first women came back to Kalumburu with half-caste kids. They came back from holidays and had white children. People mostly know who the father was, but they didn't complain. They seem to be happy, they accept the kids and enjoy them.

But I remember one Aboriginal woman in Wyndham had Aboriginal husband and one day she had a white kid in Kununurra. In the hospital, they quickly sent the child away to Perth somewhere because the husband was going to do something, kill it, so they sent it away. We never heard of it again. Mother bin going round with a ringer when her husband was away working. When the child was born, it was white. The mother had big family before she had the white kid. She had six or seven kids. Her husband didn't want to see the kid and he was pretty rough too, so the mother and the Welfare sent the child away.

There's 'nother one, pretty young Aboriginal girl from station, came to the hospital in Wyndham, but when her child was born, the child was white. I was an orderly at the hospital then. The girl was all right, but Sister told me the child was white. The girl came from Kirkimbi Station, that's all right; she was working on the station. The manager wanted her back for work and they don't mind children on stations, not in my days. Mostly, single girls get kids from the ringers.

So after independence, many part Aboriginal children were born. In those days they call 'em half-caste. Their white fathers didn't care, and their Aboriginal mothers grew 'em up. One white man in Wyndham had four children, each from a different Aboriginal mother. I don't think he helped any of them, not that I know. He was married and had other children. They had a lot of brothers and sisters in Wyndham, all right. One day, one of his Aboriginal daughters want to talk to him on the phone, but his wife answered and said, 'He hasn't got a daughter,' so they didn't try again. That wife knew about the husband have Aboriginal kids, maybe she doesn't like to hear—she was pretending, I suppose. If the whole town knows, the father doesn't have to hide anything, other people tell the wife.

One other white man in Wyndham I know, married to white wife, had a daughter from Aboriginal woman, and didn't care about her. He also had a nursery, a hardware and clothes shop and a truck. One Aboriginal girl not married had a child by him. She bin living at Lissadell Station then with the bull catcher. One weekend, the bull catcher and that girl wanted to go to Wyndham with that little child. Bull catcher must have been very drunk. There were three people in the car, all of 'em was pretty full, I think. The Toyota went like that and like that, at full speed. Maybe they had an argument, they always do when they're drunk and drive. The wheel went this way and that, the vehicle went like a zigzag, then it turned over on the left side. The little child and the girl fly out from there. The girl got killed. All got injuries. Later on, when the ambulance came, they heard a baby crying by the side in the spinifex—it was very lucky to be alive. Later police took the driver into custody and charged him and he went to jail for long time. When he came out he went away to Queensland, but came back later.

Father of that child never care, though he went to the mother's funeral. He had a wife already. He never did anything for the child. The mother died in that accident and child was sent away to Fitzroy Crossing for people there to grow her up.

She grown up now, she knows about the father. She wouldn't like to see him; they don't do that. That white wife, she has a good nature, I don't think she would've minded. Maybe the husband didn't want an Aboriginal child in his family.

None of these white men married the girls. Most of the men do nothing. They don't care for the kids or pay money to help 'em. I know these white people don't care for these kids. Only Aboriginal people grow 'em up and care for them. Most white people just don't.

There was one who did though. He's a white doctor used to live in Derby and he look after Aboriginal people. He's a very good man. Aboriginal people respect him. One Kalumburu woman lived with him for a while in Derby and they had one child, a girl. Later the woman went away with the child, but this man still cared for her and sometime the daughter go to visit him or stay there.

There are some other good white men I know in Kununurra who did marry our women properly, but not too many.

Problems in Wyndham

They had no one there to tell them; they didn't have a leader here to tell them about what alcohol is and why they go to jail before and after the drinking rights came in. They should be sick of going there. Before the drinking rights, Aboriginal people used to send kartiya to get grog for them. That's the only way they could drink. From there, police used to find out if they had bin drinking by smelling their breath when they were talking. They get 'em and put 'em away in the jail for when they have a court to find out who give them the grog.

It's easy—they could drink at home, but they just go walk in the street and that's how they get picked up. I used to live in Wyndham too, before. People that live there, they love to be put in jail all the time. Outside they got nothing to eat; that's why they like jail. People used to tell me that. They want to drink, but before that, we didn't know much about jail then, only when they start drinking and fighting in the street. Before, they used to be locked up for cattle stealing a lot, but in my time, people used to go to jail for drink. When they drink, they mostly had no rights. They got advice from Welfare, who said, 'No one stop you from drinking, go home quietly and respect everybody, just go to sleep at home.' That was about the1960s. They need someone going around and telling them, so people live normally not play cards and drink.

Before that, Aboriginal people used to go to work. Everybody had employment before the drinking rights came. Good money on the wharf! Later on, people were more interested in drinking. When they used to get paid, they went to drink then. I've seen lots of people drink, but still I never touched alcohol. I had no real idea what drink does to them.

Sometime people didn't go to work for one whole week and then lost their job. They didn't bother to go. Only long time ago, when the husband was in jail, Welfare used to look after the family. Welfare handled it. We looked for jobs and Welfare looked for vacancies for us.

This time now they got Aboriginal patrol van everywhere, going around, pick up people drunk in the street and care for them. Like in Kununurra, they got Mirriwung Patrol, but Wyndham hasn't got one. That's why in Derby they got Numbat Patrol and Broome got Kulari Patrol. Alice Springs was the first one to start, then Derby.

We asked Welfare in Wyndham, but they didn't bother. Some people got run over with the vehicle because they drunk. See, gallon-licence liquor store is in bad position. You got to go across like that all the time, while vehicle going in and going out. Even to this day, people still get run over in Wyndham because they're drunk. Nobody cares.

Outside town used to be Six Mile Hotel, now it's Community Club—you have to sign up to get in. That's the first pub you come into. At races time people used to go there, I used to go and drink there, too, later. When races time, people used to camp there everywhere. In those days people used to go back to the station with the money, but not now. People go and spend everything. Wyndham got nothing. People never change there. When they make trouble they used to take off to Oombi (Oombulgurri) to get away from the police. Long time ago, when people were causing problems, like fights and drink in the street, Welfare sent them out to Forrest River Mission to get them out of the road. Police or Welfare, tell 'em to go. People liked to go because most of them had relations there, and they could work there to earn some money. They couldn't earn anything in Wyndham, because they were on the grog all the time and there was no social security money then. The mission at Forrest River made 'em work there for a few shillings, and they were not allowed to drink there. People were also sent to stations like Dunham River Station. Now it's called Doondoon Station and is run by Aboriginal community. Ivanhoe Station was another one they were sent to and Argyle Station. Stations paid good money then. Station manager used to ring Welfare and asked for more stock boys to be sent out. There was no drink allowed in Forrest River Mission.

In Forrest River Mission, they used to have dormitory for girls only. Sometime people used to get in trouble when they sneaked up to the girls in the dormitory. In Kalumburu, they had two dormitories, one for boys and one for girls, but in Forrest River, they only had a dormitory for girls. The boys were free outside with their parents. I was there when few of the boys sneak in to the girls where they were locked up at night in Forrest River.

I'm the only one who never liked to sneak in anywhere, not used to that. They had a nurse lady sleep there with the girls at Forrest River. Even though I wanted to sneak up, I didn't like to be in trouble. Ah well, missions—you know, when you get caught, they sent our people out from Forrest River to Wyndham for punishment. I know that because I was one of the boat crew, going between Forrest River Mission and Wyndham, collecting mission stores regularly every fortnight. I didn't want to get in trouble. You know, some of these girls what I saw in Forrest River, they were very pretty girls, but I didn't bother to have one because I was interested in working and earning money. There were girls I would have liked to get, but I was too shy to even start a friendship. When I was there I used to stay with my brother, Martin, and his wife, Gwen.

There was no chance to get together with a girl in any other way in Forrest River Mission. Wherever girls go, they are always with someone else, never alone. Next day, when the superintendent find out the boys bin after the girls, they ask the boys, one by one, 'You and you and you, I want to see you in the office.' He said that after prayers in the morning and I used to know then something was wrong. The boys used to tell what they had done, couldn't deny it, because the girls knew who they were when they sneaked in at night. If the boys didn't get caught, the girls wouldn't tell, but the boys who were caught were sent away to Wyndham.

After a while, I went away to work on the stations. I wanted to find out what station work was like, out of my own free will. I asked the manager at Forrest River. He said to me, 'All right, this week I do your pay'. He was good to me because I work so hard there. From there, I left on the boat. I tell 'em like that, 'I hope you keep this barge in good order,' because I used to be one of the crew.

People learned how to drink once they were outside the mission. In Wyndham, they were free. So I was free, but I never touch alcohol then, never, because I was boss of my own. No one tell me what to do. I only think what work I want to do; that's why Father Carl find a job for me. Father Carl was the parish priest in Wyndham. Even the pretty girls when they went to town, they start to drink grog and they got used to it and never stop, which is happening to this day. Most of them died when they were still young from drinking too much or get run over by vehicle because they're drunk.

Later on, much later, I started drinking, too, but that's another story.

Turkey Creek
wine festival

One time in the 1970s, two local businessmen in Kununurra sent a 44-gallon drum of wine from Kununurra Hotel to Turkey Creek community. Only one hotel, they had then in town.

I think it was port; it was a wine anyway. Aboriginal people used to like port. It was a silver drum used for a keg, 44-gallon. It was taken there by Steve Woddell. He was the only bull catcher at the time. He own a bull catcher Toyota, you can put a 44-gallon in that, it's a tough vehicle. He was running there up and down all the time between the community and Kununurra, and he had the right vehicle.

People knew Steve Woddell. He's old pensioner now, still alive. I say hello when I see 'im, a white man, live in Kununurra for long time. He took the wine into Turkey Creek community straightaway, 'cause he used to drink with 'em. He took it for good reason: supposed to be voting for the right government. It was to encourage Aboriginal people to vote for Liberals, see.

At that time, Ernie Bridge was going to be elected. People knew him and he had property. Ernie also own a bakery in Halls Creek. Community people used to do their shopping in Halls Creek, not Kununurra. He was born in Halls Creek and was one of the Shire Presidents there. He had property at Koongie Park Station and he used to drove cattle to Wyndham from Koongie, too. Lot of boys he had working for 'im. When he was Shire President he wanted to be in politics, see, that's where many people knew him. He became the first Aboriginal man in parliament of WA, that's why drink was meant to encourage the people to vote Liberal and not Labor. So when Steve Woddell took the grog, he told 'em people at Turkey Creek, 'I got a drink here and this drink is from the Liberal party and on election you must vote for the Liberal party.'

He just took it there. He was told by the two fellas who sent him. Maybe they paid him. But people knew what's what. Aboriginal people not that silly. I think Steve Woddell was on the Labor side himself 'cause he was married to Aboriginal woman. Aboriginal people was very glad to have that drink, but they really knew who they was going to vote for. They had a few and some got drunk, but they drink the wine first and then they vote for Ernie Bridge after, and Steve Woddell took the drum back.

Ernie won that election. People vote for Ernie Bridge 'cause he is Aboriginal, he know more about them because he is one. They knew him well and he knows them, they trusted him. We voted for him in Kununurra, too. I hear the story in Kununurra many times about that keg. When people drink they enjoy it very much, 'specially 'cause it was free. If I lived there, I would have drunk it myself. They were all happy, they talk a lot about it after, and it was a big joke. Long after voting was done, they still enjoy the story afterwards. From there it went around the whole of the Kimberley. They thought it was a wonderful story, even in the city they had heard it and laugh about it very much. The Liberal Party was the one that give the Aboriginal people drinking rights. Before, they had to have a dog licence to be allowed to drink in a hotel.

Though Aboriginal people got the vote finally in 1967, I wasn't on the roll for quite a while. I had no idea about electoral rolls; nobody in the remote communities was on the roll for long time. I think in Kalumburu, they started to put people on the roll when the mission was still there in Father Sanz' time. He said to people you can vote for this one or that one, he didn't tell 'em who to vote for, he just told 'em they had a choice. Later, someone from the government in Wyndham went and put people on the electoral roll.

I was in Kununurra when I wanted to get on the roll and I ask the girls in the Walkabout shop, who were good friends of Ernie Bridge. They help me fill out the form and get it to the post office to get on the electoral roll.

I was in Kalumburu once when it was voting time in the '96 state election. Two white politicians came up, one from Derby; 'nother one was from Karratha,. This one from Karratha, he was a sitting member. He was driven out to Wulngga (McGowan Island Beach) where we live. We exactly tell 'im, show 'im the place, the bad conditions people were living there, about the housing short- age in Kalumburu. He walked in there and said, 'I might try to do something about it', and he would let us know. We heard fuck-all from him, he didn't care, he never try, he wouldn't even let us know. I wrote to the Premier about the housing in Kalumburu. At least he wrote back a letter, but this politician never answered me.

He and the other Derby man stood outside Kalumburu office to talk to the people. I don't know what they said, like you do this and I might help you. Not many people came to listen. Some, the old people, think he was all right. They asked me, they said, 'He looks like a good person, we vote for this one'. I said nothing, because people in the communities they mostly haven't got a fair idea of what the politicians are like. Politicians always look good when they come, I myself can't tell the difference. They fly in and out, don't say nothing much, they only come to see the place and enjoy the journey. That money for the flight is wasted. Kalumburu people don't see that, but I do know, because I live outside most of the time.

Too much fire

Long time ago, this Kimberley bush wasn't damaged by fire much, but now bush burn nearly all the time. My people did make fire, but only certain places to cook and for hunt—that was really controlled burning. Or when people travel, they sometime light a fire to let others know they're coming. Then they put it out. People didn't let fire burn out of control, not like today. They use it proper way. Forest right around was nice and green where everybody enjoyed it. This time lately people make fire everywhere, no one is there to tell 'em, or they don't listen. Some think it is a good fun to start a fire for nothing. Nowadays the community council should take proper care to protect the bush and the environment.

I started this story while I live at Wulngga in 1996/97. At that time there was a huge fire burning on the other side of the bay, and this is what I said then: This fire that's burning now across Mission Bay is worse, it's bin burning from the start when we came to live here at Wulngga, near Kalumburu, three months ago.

You can see it burn for miles. Someone lights it, you can tell. I see people drive around mostly on weekend, throw the match while they drive, maybe a whole box of matches and then just drive off. We seen people make fire in the road when their vehicle broke down, parents sitting down right by the roadside, their children went around with fire sticks and light the bush here and there, wherever they wanted, and parents never said nothing. That fire bin burn for long time now and far into the bush. Each day we go past it and see more trees burn.

The fire opposite bin burning long time. Night-time we can see a smoke and the fire glow all the way, all along that coast line, never stop, a red, red glow all night across Mission Bay. We watch it start from Monger Creek one weekend and then it carry on and on 'til the end of that peninsula, a long, long way. For three months it burns that entire bush. At sunset time, smoke cover the sun, the sun look more beautiful with the smoke over it, but it's not good.

I don't know why the people want a land claim for it. If they burn the bush all the time, no cattle, no kangaroo will be left, except fish you can't hurt, it's in the water. By the time I get my land it will be burnt. If the bush burns all the time, each year, finally country will turn into a desert. That's what I say then.

Later, in 1998, when I live at Oomarri in the dry season, we saw too many fires all the time, huge, bad fires, fierce fire that burn for week after week, so that again we bin see the sun become red like blood each night at going down time. I smell kooro (Cypress Pine) burning for miles; it was that strong, the fire. After we drove for miles and miles through black charcoal bush—nothing alive in it, even the pandanus at the creeks are dead now.

People need an education about fire, they need Aboriginal people to explain the damage the fire can do, and how soon there'll be nothing left. One match can destroy big bush. It take a long time to grow. Short while ago they sent some white people up to Kalumburu to talk to community 'bout fire danger. Later, in Kununurra, I heard that the people in Kalumburu eat all the food and don't want to listen to the talk after. The old people know 'bout fires but young ones don't take any notice of them any more.

I also saw paper leaflets come from the city about fire danger in Kimberley, and how much bush burn each year. That information's not easy to read and understand for Kalumburu people. It's meant for white people. It's high words in that paper, my people don't talk like that, and so it's wasted. White people mostly think what's good for them must be good enough for us, but it doesn't always work that way. We know what works best for our people, but white people who make rules, don't want to find out. That's why they give us things made for white people and wonder why it won't work. I think some Aboriginal people who know how, could make a video that would teach people about fire and take care of environment. People like watching videos and Aboriginal people can tell 'em in a lingo they understand—they would learn that way.

When I live in Kalumburu, when the Wet came, there was not much bush fruit could be found, only very few bush apples. Most of the bush fruit get ripe in the Wet. That's because fire destroy the flowers and young fruit on the tree and when time come to eat it, there's nothing left. It doesn't even have chance to grow in the first place. Before we used to find plenty each year.

When we lived in the mission and went in the bush, we didn't light any bad fires, we only light fire to cook or boil something. We took the tea and boil the billy, certain time we light fire, they didn't teach us about fire; we know it ourselves. When we were small, we learn from our old people. They told us how to be careful, they teach us not to make fire without permission, and make it in a clear spot so fire don't get away. Your belonging might get burnt; make fire in creek bed or on the rocks near a river.

In the Kimberley nowadays, some tourists are careless, too, and fire gets away. Some people throw cigarette butts out the vehicle and a fire starts. One day some tourists try to smoke some fish inside their tent. Fire got out and race around that whole camping area. All the tall dry cane grass burn, and we all had to get bucket and cooking pots to get it under control. We manage to put it out, so other tents didn't catch fire. Lucky we had enough water from the bore. The two fellas lost their tent, all their clothes and brand new fishing gear—we all felt sorry for them, their holiday was finished.

Some fires are caused by lightning, too, but then the rain might be not far away. It's the people mostly that don't take care.

Lately, here in the city in 1999, I see many people stand up and fight for their forest down south that the government wants to cut down to make more money. Nobody burns that bush there; looks like the government wants to finish it altogether by logging it all away. I just wish people in the Kimberley could see that the bush in our region is in great danger too.

My Kwini camp
for remembrance

My father Piurungei Chalarimeri stay in that Kwini camp only for short time. I didn't know his age then, but I see in a document now that the mission staff estimate his age to be seventy-five in those days. They wouldn't know for sure, 'cause Aboriginal people didn't need a calendar. When father was there, he used to sit under the big *winjibut* tree, the ironwood tree that made lots of shade. He lived under that tree. In those days they just had humpies then, the huts were built later.

When my father was there, we sit down and talk. Sometime he was away hunting with a spear, and he gave me kangaroo meat when he had any. Or he organised meeting for the people, tell 'em what's bin happening this way or that way. He also used to help many people because he knew bush medicine. He used to travel a lot all over the place.

Kwini camp was there while I was in the dormitory. Later, when I was big, I live in the cottages in the community with my brother, where Augustin camp used to be.

After I left mission, I work all the time away from Kalumburu. I often used to think, one day, if I live in Kalumburu, I want to have a house in the old Kwini camp, where my people used to live.

I was working for APB (Agricultural Protection Board), you know, on a donkey shoot. I was starting from Kalumburu. Boss used to ask me, 'Do you want to start at Halls Creek or Kalumburu?' I always said, 'In Kalumburu.'

When I go there on the government truck, I always pass along that road that go past the Kwini camp place. Nobody live there now, they all gone. Each time I drive past, I always think once my people live there in that Kwini camp. As you come into the community from the Gibb River Road, Kwini camp is on the left side. You cross over that little creek, that Woraro Creek, there's a paddock on the left and on that land, once some people of my tribe lived. Inside that paddock there's a small tin shack, it's still there today. The people that didn't like to live in the mission itself, the old people, they lived there a few minutes away from the mission buildings, but they weren't part of the mission. It was very good there, lots of shady trees and big winjibut tree, the ironwood tree.

There were about four or five of those tin shacks in the camp. Mission build that for people, I think. I used to go there a lot, many Kwini people live there when I came to Kalumburu from the bush as a child. This time, when I bin away and after I came back, I saw it all deserted. Only one hut is still there. I never had my own place while I work all these years, an' I bin away from Kalumburu all that time. I was thinking I wanted to have my own place and it would be nice to have a little house there, in that spot, because my people lived there. That's why I wanted to live there when I go to Kalumburu. Even my father lived there and old Joe Puruan', because he was Kwini too, an' a good number of them lived there. They used to walk to the mission up and down and to the Kulari camp. The old man that disappeared, Yogin, he lived there all the time, too. Kulari camp was the other side of the river.

I used to go to the camp as a child, and even after, when I was living outside for a while and visited Kalumburu. When I was small, I visit the camp for a day at the weekend; sometime I go in the middle of the week, in the afternoon. I had to go and ask Father Boniface if I could go. He said, 'Yes, you can go there, come back before dark, before your supper.' He was a good man and I always do that.

I go and sit down there, have a talk. Sometime they used to dance there, sometime the old people used to tell me story. I used to stay for a while and then go back to the dormitory. That Kwini camp's the only place I want in Kalumburu, because all my people used to live there. That was my Kwini world, for remembrance. I used to go up and down there, visit them; I couldn't do any more. If it didn't exist, the Kwini camp, I wouldn't have heard many of the stories, and I wouldn't know much.

The Kwini camp was free, no fence. It went all the way to Laoar Creek. But in 1996 I saw mission had put fence around it. At that time I look around for a place to stay there. I wanted a small block where the Kwini camp used to be. Didn't need the whole paddock, just a small piece. Enough for a house. I still had my mind on that. I think, might as well build a house where I want it. It was mission land now, 'cause mission had a fence around it. One day the Bishop came and I had in my mind to ask him if I could build a small house there. I think if I had asked Bishop Jobst, it would've bin easier. He was the Bishop before that. We written letter to this Bishop now and explain it in writing and the reason why I want that land. When Bishop Saunders came, we asked to see him and gave him that letter. He looked at it and tell me I can put in a Native Title claim elsewhere, not on mission land. I said there is nothing on that land now and I only want a small piece, not the whole lot. He tell me it's mission land, and he has something planned for it. He tell me he will think about it and let me know. He took my letter with him.

That was in 1996 and now is 1999. I am still waiting. I don't think he treat me with respect. When we get that letter to the Bishop, he didn't respond like he said he would. He didn't let me know. Well, I think that's not right, that's all. Mission got the best land in Kalumburu by the river; they only have few people in the mission now. Long time they used to feed the people, now they sell some of the fruit they grow in the community shop. For tiny bananas, we pay one dollar each! And they grow 'em in the mission.

Long time ago, Mission had their land given by government. Nobody ask us. I say Mission can have that, because they did look after us, but that little piece of land that I want, Bishop was no good about it.

Tourists in my country

The tourist season in the Kimberley start in June, though some people come early in May. If we have a big Wet, road is still too soft and vehicles get bogged easy. When the road is wet and people drive over it with the four-wheel-drive, they make the road worse. The wheels turn the mud over and over, road gets churned up, and the more you try, the more it gets softer and more vehicles get stuck. One time when we travel on the Gibb River Road, we come to a creek that run across the track. There are no bridges or anything like that. The tracks up in that country cross many rivers and creeks. That's why, in the Wet, nobody can travel there at all except might be by plane, if airstrip isn't too soggy, cause then the plane get bogged. We couldn't cross over that creek because a big fuel truck was sitting in the middle and couldn't move back or front. He was stuck in the mud and water. It held us up; we had to camp there the night cause we couldn't get past with our vehicle. Many roads in the Kimberley turn into a river in the Wet, you can see it from the air, look like a proper river for miles. Some of the dips in the road stay full of water well into the dry season, and one or two are so deep, you may have to find a way round 'em.

June is the best time to go because most tourists like to see waterfall still running where the gorges are, like Calvin Gorge, or

Mitchell River, Emma Gorge, King George waterfalls—that's my country—and lots of others.

Years ago, road wasn't built, but now since we have the road, many tourists come every year. Just a little while ago I work with the tourists at Wulngga—McGowan Island Beach is white man name—north of Kalumburu. Proper Aboriginal name is *Wulngga*, name of a tree there. I didn't know it was that name, 'til one of the old people told us. My sister and brother-in-law build that place up. When my brother-in-law was still alive, the place was very good and happy. Tourist bin enjoying coming there for holiday. I live there for a while in '96 because my brother-in-law became sick. I look after the place and the tourists. Later on we couldn't live there any more, when my brother-in-law passed away.

Wulngga is 20 km north from Kalumburu and Timor Sea is all around. Tourists can go to two places for camping—to Honeymoon Beach run by Lesley French family (they're Kalumburu people), and to Wulngga, on Mission Bay. On the opposite side of the bay, you can see the Kul mountain and behind there is Kingana and Truscott Airbase a bit further on. That's all Kulari country. The King Edward River flows into Mission Bay near the Longhani Landing. Place to visit nearby is Pago, that's where Kalumburu Mission started early this century. It was called Drysdale River Mission then.

When some tourists arrive, they like the place and come again. They tell friends and more and more tourists come, even from overseas. My brother-in-law charged them $10 a night for one vehicle, camping fee to pay for water and facilities. He knew there was a bit of a soak in the bush nearby, and he put bore casing down and a pump. That's how he got a very good water supply there. Water comes pure from the ground and it taste pretty good. He laid plastic pipes, big ones from the soak to the camping area, and he put one water tank up on a hill for pressure. Mango trees were planted for shade and fruit, and every dry season they got fertilised with heaps of fish scraps from the daily fishing. He bought a boat to take tourists fishing and sightseeing, and he didn't charge much. Many people that bin there once like to come back. They like the bush and the sea, and some even like the Aboriginal people.

My brother-in-law had a friend, George. He is a very good man and he work with us for the tourists each year. When I work there, I take tourists sightseeing and fishing at Malinjarr—King Edward River Gorge.

At Malinjarr, you need a little boat because it's shallow there in the dry season. When I stay in the mission, we used to have fish trap there. Mission built it long time ago; is not there any more now. You cannot swim in the gorge because big, big crocodile live there. I took notice long time ago; the rock in the gorge is smooth. Every year in the Wet the river rise about ten meters or more, and run through there very fast, and carry lots of wood and sticks, that make the rock smooth.

The beach at Wulngga is lovely with rocks on the side, good for fishing. You can have a bit of a swim there but beware of crocodiles, and other things. Some days, early morning time, in the sand, we see track of a big croc that bin sleeping there in the night. Lots of sharks in the bay too, and turtles, and dolphins, and even dugong we seen there.

Many tourists are good, but some don't know how to do things proper way, and some just don't care. One thing, there's the rubbish for a start. I think people should take their own rubbish back out. I seen this done in 'nother place like Bungle Bungles. They don't even have bins there.

At Wulngga, they got a rubbish tip dug out there in the middle of the bush. It bin dug with the machine, so we can drive in and dump all the rubbish there, left by the tourists. Well, before I thought it was a good idea, now I change my mind, cause I see how it spoil the bush and things leak into soil and make it bad.

When I went to my country, Oomarri, that's where we discover lot of rubbish there, in very remote place, hard to get to. You just never know where tourists might go and what they do. If they responsible, all right, but I see some don't care. I know that tourists even discover burial places hidden in our bush, and I worry they may disturb it. The white law that's supposed to protect Aboriginal sites, is weak and doesn't help, government don't care much about our sites in the bush.

Rubbish is like a disaster when you see it in a community like Kalumburu. There, today, they still don't have a proper tip that is managed well, so rubbish blow about when wind comes and rain, and half the rubbish wash down the road. Tourist make it worse. Even in the camping ground, some leave things lie around, meat bone, fish bone, scales, insides, heaps of oyster shells, cans, plastic bottles, anything they leave. Some people when they go for toilet in the bush, you see paper everywhere lying around. Should bury everything deep or rain will flood it out all over the place later.

Long time Aboriginal people used to cook fish in the skin. We still do when we can because skin is good to eat with the fish, scale get burnt, that's why we don't clean and scale the fish. We know nuns clean it like that in the mission, but we cook it different, guts an' all. They got fat in 'em that make it good. When they cook with the guts, guts are easy to come out, and cooked guts don't smell. We ask people not to clean fish on the beach because that bring dogs, and dog bring shark and croc too.

Some people take too much fish, some I seen come with freezers and want to load it full up. If you catch too much fish in one area, nothing will be left. Oysters, too, some people take many as they can there, not worry 'bout leaving some for others.

People shouldn't leave fishing line along the beach and rocks. Sea birds get tangled in it and then can't fly. Or it gets into the water and sea animals get caught in it. They drown or get strangled. Long time ago, if they get caught in string line, they can chew that. We used to use string fishing line before. On the coil was written St Paul. It was strong fishing line; salt didn't affect it. It doesn't get caught easily, not like nylon line, what is light—string line is much safer.

The sea is very beautiful all along the Kimberley coast and people like to go in boats. Trouble is that boats make pollution with the engine oil and I can see it in the water—see oil scum float on top. Tide can take it out but when it come back, the tide might turn it up in 'nother place. Oil can't disappear and it's no good for fish and birds.

I like to see people respect our rock art and sites in the bush, not take photos without asking. I seen one place where Aboriginal people put fence around a site, forget where that is. There are white people take photos of my people's rock art and then make it into cards and sell 'em. They don't even ask for permission, they just do it.

Feral cats are big problem in the bush, and some tourist they feed the feral cats. They could take 'em home instead. Lot of feral cats there in the Kimberley. I seen one that had got hold of a bird, it was a pretty parrot. Pity I didn't have a gun, I could've shot that cat. By the time we stopped the vehicle and jump out, cat disappeared. We run into many when go walkabout there, and they breed more and more. Cats eat little birds, and small animals like lizards and other native animals, some of them. Not many left now.

I think cats came from overseas on ships first, then later white people bring 'em as pets. On the ships they come long time ago before white people came, they eat the rats and that's how they got here. They sneak away from the ship and land like everybody else. They hunt to live.

Well, this time our Aboriginal people should be trained to manage tourist when they come to communities. They could take 'em out in the boat, fishing or sightseeing, they know the bush and can tell stories—that way it keep our culture going and our people can earn a living. I like to show some tourists some of my country 'cause I think they might understand Aboriginal people better after I tell 'em about it. People that are not Aboriginal in this country mostly don't know much about us.

Tourism can be good for communities 'cause Aboriginal and white people can get to know one another better. Good few tourists come up and ask my partner and me questions about Aboriginal people and things. I can see that most don't know much at all and I think it's good they come and ask.

Native title—we bin waiting long enough

Well, one time ago they used to talk about this Native Title come in, you know. This Native Title and Land Rights meeting is new to me, in my days I didn't go. I don't say I wasn't interested, but I had no time, all the time I was working.

I couldn't live with members of my family like other people do—like sit down there, play cards, lose money, and if they want to, they drink. I couldn't do that. My life would be ruined, easy as that. Living among brothers and sisters, their families and friends like they do, you get nowhere. I could have joined them in those days. What could I do if I live with them—I have to do what they do! Well, I just don't like living with everybody like that. I thought better off live in another place, I might get somewhere with it. When I went away, that doesn't mean I stay away from everybody for good; I went to visit them.

Some of my brothers and sisters were working at Forrest River Mission then. Now it's called Oombulgurri. They used to work but when they got money, they go to town and drink. I see them there at the Six Mile Hotel back in 1970s. Before they go to town, they gamble. They leave some money behind for family and then go. People used to gamble all the time, there's no end to that, back from the 1960s, wherever they live, they used to play cards.

When people went in and out of town, that's what they learned—how to play cards from outside to inside. In the mission, they start sneaking away to play, mission didn't allow them. They sneak away from work without letting the mission people know, make things no good for everybody. Mission didn't allow gambling because it keeps people from work and it leads some men to sell their wife. So if someone win a lot of money, a husband could send his wife to that person to get money, like a prostitute, long as he give you the money. The money run out, the woman goes back to her husband.

I see myself gambling is no good. Sometime they ask me to play but I said, 'I never play cards.' I was frightened of losing one shilling. I used to be only interested in gambling on a racehorse or charity tickets. Nowadays I also buy lotto tickets. Cards is no good in many ways because it make people sit down and gamble their money away. It was no good then and it is no good to this day.

Cards was the one that don't make 'em go to work, that was the start. When I went out to stations to work I see people play cards, gamble all their money away. That's when I first saw them play cards. They play cards on stations long before the '60s.

Aboriginal station people learn it from the white people that play poker for money. On the station I used to see the Aboriginal people gamble all their money away and then wait 'til their next pay comes. We used to get monthly pay. Manager don't mind if people play cards when they knock off work, even out in the stock camp. They don't care long as people do their work. They never play in working hours, only at night they used to play.

It's different on stations because people are on the move from camp to camp with the stockmen moving the cattle, so people only played at night or Sundays. People didn't play cards at smoko time or lunchtime. They left their cards in the camp, they wasn't interested in playing in the day.

They wasn't allowed to drink in those days. No grog allowed on the station even after citizen right. The rule was still 'no alcohol'. They could always go to town to drink, even the manager. Don't remember seeing managers drink on the station because station take the rules of the owner, just like in the mission, the Bishop makes the rules.

'Cause I don't stay with family much, I wasn't around when land claim meetings are held. Some people don't realise why I didn't go to the Kimberley Land Council (KLC) meetings then. They didn't see I was working all the time. When this Native Title business come in around 1992, I was still working with the Agriculture Department in Kununurra. That's why some people think I'm not interested in land claim. The KLC didn't see that only if I didn't work I could be at the meetings. Might be they don't understand I have to work for a living, too. A few Aboriginal people who work did go to meetings, not many. When my job run out I used to live somewhere else. I moved around working all the time. But whether I go to meetings or not, Oomarri is still my country. I could be in England or somewhere else; I still belong there (Oomarri).

Finally, I heard that word Mabo very fast too. Before I never heard of Eddie Mabo. I knew he live in Queensland. They said he was from Murray Island. I said, 'That is in the Torres Strait somewhere, what's that got to do with us over here?' That's what I thought. Took me long time to understand, to know what Mabo means. People talked about it a lot and some thought it was good to join him.

I know some people went to KLC meetings, but I said I am still working. It's very important all right, but meeting was always in working time and took long time to finish. People who work could not always go to meetings, take time off. I couldn't go—mine was a different case. I was working in the bush. I can see clear it won't work for me, even though it was my land they talk about. I did think about it, but I couldn't miss work, I was on the payroll. I couldn't take overtime, there's no overtime in the bush, so I couldn't get time-in-lieu for meetings.

KLC people say I don't go to meetings—they don't understand why. I had a good reason not to go, I earned good money. I said I can go at the weekend but not when I work. It isn't easy for Aboriginal people to get good jobs.

Later I could go to meeting sometime, but it's still not easy. I'm not used to meetings like that. Because I couldn't go before, some things I understand but some it's a bit hard. By the time I attend meeting I can only see halfway what they talk about. As for me, I never bin and some people, specially the kartiya, talk in high words I can't understand. Even the chairman of the KLC, some of us can't always follow his meaning. He come and talk to us at Oombulgurri. 'Nother thing, when we go to meetings it seems they talk the same thing all the time and we don't know when it's going to be settled. It's no good for us.

The high words we can't follow. We don't ask; people just let it go. We're afraid of asking because the kartiya and lawyers mightn't like to be asked again. They mightn't like repeating it a few times, and even then we mightn't understand the answer, so people prefer to say nothing, let it pass. You can't expect me to understand it all. It worries people when they can't follow. Others don't understand much, either. I know that for a fact, only few people know what's really going on. I also say that we traditional owners don't get told everything we should be by the KLC.

Well, from my point of view, I ask how many people go to meetings in my Balangarra Native Title claim group that are born in my country? Some that go to meetings were not even born there, only others in their family. I am the only one that was born there, the old people told me. Even Father Sanz in the mission, he told me, 'That's your country there.' It should be the owner who belong there, no others. I think one or two of my brothers are born there, but they're gone now. I was born in the bush in that country, and I live in the bush 'til I was about six or seven.

There are diamonds in my country. Mining companies bin there for long time now looking, and they found some. I heard that the company gave traditional owners some money and the KLC bin hanging on to it for years. When I'm at the meeting, I always think some people are there only for the money they think they might get out of it, otherwise they mightn't go; they wouldn't bother 'cause they don't understand about the land any more. Lately KLC give that money to the traditional owners, but I only got very little. I heard others bin getting much more, I don't know why or how. Don't know how the KLC work it all out. I don't know how that money was shared out. It was money from the mining company and we should all have got a proper account of how people got what amount.

Once they tasted flour, tea and sugar in the mission, some of our people didn't worry about the country for a while. People still knew their country even though they were sitting down in the mission being fed. Only later they start to think about their country again. My brother Monba wanted to go back to our country long ago and stay there, that's why he ask me to go with him.

In those days, nobody know about mining companies and how they come and explore—look for things and dig holes in the ground. Tanganyika Mine came first in the Kimberley; later on CRA was there, then Stockdale, now Striker.

People had no idea mining companies could spoil the whole place, take things out of the ground, destroy the nature of our country. We didn't really know much what bin happen outside the mission, how the whole country was getting full of kartiya. That there's a big government now, telling people what to do. We didn't know what government is. We only knew the little place we bin grown up; we didn't know anything about outside like town, city, buses, trains. We heard about courthouse and to be in trouble, that's all we knew because police come to Kalumburu look for people that make trouble and some that don't make trouble. We didn't know what bin happen at the other end. People that come back from prison they didn't tell us about what they did and how they bin in jail. They didn't like to talk about it; there's no reason to talk about it.

The missionaries tell us 'bout European Spanish history and who discovered the country. That's our country they talk about and we bin here long time, not like them, they just come lately. In those days, people didn't realise all what's bin happen to our land. They lose everything. Only later they turn around and realise they can do something for themselves and the land what bin taken away from them.

Our land in North Kimberley is still there if people want to go back. Only mining mob there now. There was always some of our people that keep going to their country and even stay there. My father spent lot of time going up and down in our country when he wasn't working. Mostly he live in the bush. Later my brother, Brian, was the first one who went back to the land and others follow him.

Monba, I used to call him by his bush name—he used to call me Mungala, he was the first man there who had a Toyota; written on it was 'King George River', middle of '70s that was. He was the first one to go back with all the children. I took him to Kununurra for a ride when I own a car one time. He told me he wanted me there on our land, but I was working. He wanted me to go to Oomarri and build a place and stay. He told me 'That's our land, and I want to go back there before anything happen to me,' that's what he said, 'Anytime you finish work, you come there.'

I wanted to go but had nothing to go in and he was out there. Or I was away working; I never get around making arrangements. I just let it go for a while, see what happens. I was worried I might get stuck for a lift out there and I couldn't get back easily to my job. To work in my country that's very remote; you got to get off the job in town altogether. Others they could stay there at Oomarri because of the way they lived before with everybody else, they didn't work like me. I am like that; I didn't want to be on the dole. I was on a salary—salary was big money, different to the dole. I was on the big one, you're not heading for the small one then, other people may not see that. It was not 'til later I heard about this Mabo first time. I thought something good might come of it, but Monba had died then.

When you think about it now, when you look back, it's just like looking at the big picture. When you older you see lot of things drawn behind, you don't see that before, that big picture. I should have gone to the land, should've went there because the big picture draws that, and then you realise you should've gone there in the first place. It would have bin better I had gone. If I missed out on a salary, I missed out. We had to know our land—money, it just goes. I should've went there. If you haven't got money the land is always there. We are lucky in the Kimberley, but many Aboriginal people cannot go back to their land any more, it's all full, no space left for them, because other people are on it.

Today I like to go to the land; today it's different. Today it's bit easier for me, but you still have to know how to survive, you can't beat the land, but the land can beat you. You need a good vehicle that's all; the country is so remote and very isolated. In the Wet you can't move around. If we want the land we need a vehicle, we can't go walking there any more.

The Native Title claim meetings still go on and on. I don't know where we're heading. When I go to the meeting now, it still cost money for me because I don't live close by. Only the people that make the meeting get paid. We get nothing from it, not a cent, you know. I could tell 'em 'You gett'n paid to come here, we don't—you working for yourself, for your pocket, we get nothing, not a cent.' They don't give us back our land yet either, it takes too long, people give up. We bin waiting long enough, too long.

People bin going to meetings six years already. We might get the land when we die; we don't see nothing now. So many of my people have died already and they don't all have children that come after them. Not many left, hardly any of the old people left to go to meeting now. They the ones who know everything, once they're gone that's it. Most are gone now; something should be done. It's the government rules that are wrong. I believe the Kimberley Land Council should be finished altogether. Mining companies should work direct with us. Come together with us without the KLC. It works good in other places, some of my friends tell me about it. I think we better off without them, more better for Aboriginal people to get somewhere. Just give us our land, what's left—we're the owners and we wait long enough.

What's going to happen when they dam the Fitzroy River?

Beautiful country it was, I used to work there. The place was good, that's why I was working there. When the Ord River was dammed, everything was lost.

It is a big property. It goes right up to Northern Territory border. The land was pretty good; a big open area with lot of cattle in it, a flat plain, but the mountain wasn't far away. We used to call that Mount Misery or Grasshopper Hill, don't know what the Mirriwung people call it. The place was very nice and clear.

When you look to the Ord River across the flat plain, the sunrise was beautiful in the morning. The Ord River comes from Purnululu, all the way it goes to the sea. When you fly over there, you can see it. Bush name for Argyle homestead they used to call 'em *Bilbilji*. A bit higher that way up from the creek there was the old house. They lived there first, away from the mountain. New homestead is long way from there, I'll show you, I take you there, one day. The old one is flooded. They build a new one further away. It's higher up, not flooded.

Our Aboriginal camp used to be called *Ngalwooriwoori*. I forget the other bush names we had for other places. That camp had a tin shed for single men quarters. It was a very basic, long building.

Men had just one room, like dongas, made out of steel, pretty hot. When I was working there, I put timber there, in the ceiling. It was cooler then. By gee, the heat go through that corrugated iron there, no fan, no air-conditioning. For electricity there was a generator, I used to go and start 'em up.

Ringers live in the quarters, which was built out of concrete. It was good house, that one, you know. Where Aborigines live no white people go there. Even the half-caste camp was 'nother side, the part-Aboriginals, they didn't mix with us people, only with the ringers when they work with them. Part-Aborigines weren't allowed to mix with Aboriginal people that had no white blood in them. That was a law that time.

Sunday we used to go hunting. There was a lot of shade down the creek, big paperbarks. We used to walk long way through Benn River Gorge, water used to come down from it. Benn River is near the homestead. The main river is the Ord.

Special Aboriginal sites were along the big riverside. The Ord River come round in a circle like that and rock painting are all on one side, 'nother painting past the spillway. Near the homestead there were no paintings, no rocks there to paint on.

More paintings were up where the Ord River comes in, sunset way where the Ord passes through the valley, where people used to live there long time ago. Old man used to tell me, 'That's where more paintings are.' It's flooded now, all gone. People used to go there, round the other side of the river when it was all dry. You see, the Ord used to be dry when it didn't rain. You could cross over in the sand. It took us 'til lunchtime to walk there from the homestead. It got lot of paperbark in it like Laoar Creek in Kalumburu. Aboriginal people used to go there when they had time off work, and along the creek near the Aboriginal camp, they used to have corroboree. Country was very beautiful, with lots of kangaroos and emus. Sunday we used to go shooting not far away and lot of fish there, too, in a gorge.

Then I heard they was going to dam it. Bulldozer came and knocked everything down there, trees and all. I lived in Kununurra when they build the dam wall. One day, I went there to see it. All was pretty dry. They were building the dam wall up stone by stone. When I saw it, it was still at the bottom.

The Aboriginal people didn't really understand fully what was going to happen. They only thought this house is going to be moved to some other place, we never thought about anything else, about the flooding. Only slowly we find out. Construction people came and talked on the station. At that time, nobody thought much about it. We never thought about how everything would be spoilt. Nobody had any idea. I didn't either. We didn't know, nobody knew, we never thought it would turn out like that.

The Ord River Dam in Kununurra was the first one they built, the other one in the '70s came later to support all the farmers. Kimberley Research Station that was there already had its own water pump, they didn't need any dam, they had their own water. We only knew of the old Ivanhoe homestead that got flooded near Kununurra, when they built a dam there to keep the water balanced. We had no idea of the Argyle Dam flooding everything. We had no idea.

I wasn't there when it was flooded. I was in Wyndham. All that is Mirriwung country, they didn't know, not at that time. We Aboriginal people were never known to talk about anything much at that time, you know. You take notice now. It's different these days. People did not know in those days. Nowadays people can stand up for themselves. Long time ago, we cannot say or do anything because white people was ruling. This time all right, everybody can talk against each other, they can demonstrate. Now the white people can be slowed down, they think more a little bit.

Nothing was done by the Aboriginal people before because we didn't know about our land rights or any other rights. We didn't say anything. Nothing was mentioned about the rock art 'cause people had no say. Aborigines knew lots of sites but they didn't tell the white people. They didn't want them to see because some were sacred sites.

I was thinking lot about the station. I used to live there and feed the pigs and chooks and cattle. We used to go walkabout, have picnics, wonderful time we had before dam was built. I remember the house and the landscape was beautiful. I used to think if no rain falls and when it is all dry, we can see that country again. Now I know we can't, it's gone forever.

When they opened that Argyle Homestead museum, everyone was invited. One old fella ask me, 'Tonight is a truck going in if you want to go.' Straight 'way I said no, because I didn't bother to go back there. I knew they would talk about the olden days. I didn't want to hear about it. I was sad for the place too, sad for the place, because I work there for a long time myself.

The people was telling me the water came at night, they heard it come. Someone went with the helicopter to pick up one stockman, a boundary man, an Aboriginal man. He let the bridle go and the saddle and they picked him up and let the horse go. It was all right it can swim. When the flood water came they went to the old road and cut all the fences out so the cattle could go away, cattle can swim that's all right, it's calm not like running water. All the horse gear was lost, saddle room still had lot of saddle, few people dive in and get saddle for themselves. One kartiya, Howard Young, got one truck there from under the water. He built a raft and got it out.

The Fitzroy River is a beautiful area too, especially where there is lots of deep water, everlasting water. I don't know what they're going to do with it when they dam it. Mosquito breed up then in swamps created by the flood, and plants will grow that are not there now, no good plants just like that cabangi weed in Kununurra. The Shire try to get rid of it for years, they still can't and the Shire spray in the street for insects.

During the Wet, it's no good near the river now since the dam is there. Crocs come, even some salties. The dam creates all sort of dangerous things. Crocs, they can go over the dam now. They can walk. Before, there was no water in the dry time. The crocs never got that far, they are there now because of the dam, because there is water there all the time.

They shouldn't dam the Fitzroy River because people lose their hunting ground, and fishing areas. They fish a lot there. They couldn't go any more if dam water is there and no room for the people to go goanna hunting. You can't do much fishing if it's flooded. Without the water you can survive. A dam creates a lot of water but it creates a lot of flooding too. When it's running all the time, the water is kept on the land. It might make it different because the water doesn't flood that much. Perhaps the station people look at it that way as they lose a bit of cattle there in the floods.

They always talk about jobs for Aboriginal people when they want to do this kind of thing. When the jobs come out, always the white people take it first, they are the first ones and Aboriginal people are left behind, that's what I know. When they say they create jobs—instead of Aboriginal people, white people take it all.

I don't know what they're going to do with their rock art. They can't move it anywhere else. If they dam the Fitzroy River, once it's flooded, it's flooded, nothing you can do. Dams are good only for certain places. At the Fitzroy, they had sheep farm there one time and they grow rice, but they didn't need to dam it. They built a wall to bring the water around where it is needed. Perhaps they should build a pipeline where the gorge is and run the water to where the farms are. Maybe a lot of other things they can do to get the water, but not drown that Dimond Gorge. I think they should build a canal to get the water from the Fitzroy but from lower down stream, so that nobody's land gets drowned. There is a lot of water still wasted there that flows into the sea, and that could be used for farming.

I wouldn't like my country at Oomarri (at King George River) flooded. The Fitzroy belong to the people that live on that country. There are a lot of Bunuba tribe people there, all that area around the Fitzroy is full of Aboriginal people, Mount Anderson, Halls Creek, Derby, all the stations too, full of Aboriginal people. They got rock art there, too, sacred sites. People go hunting there, yes, 'specially older people still alive. They the ones to go to the bush all the time, they camp there all the time. The younger generation come there too, they drive, they cut fire wood, hunt. They got no other way, they like to go place where they have connection to their land. People are used to go same place, 'nother place don't suit 'em, that's not their country. They have to go to the land they belong to. They can't go 'nother place because the ancestors lived there, people was born there, they hunt there and survived there.

Your connection to your country is very important. You feel good about the country that you belong to. The feeling comes out in the life of the country you belong to. The land gives people food to live, and you go and camp there because the land is important to a person. You can hunt somewhere else and then take the food to your land and cook it there. Sometime you think of the story that come out from the land itself, Lalai (Dreamtime) story, like you born there, remember what bin happen, how the world was made, how the river is coming, like the painting on the rocks. When you are away for a while, might be you forget, but now and then you think about your country, and feel you might think of going back there, because your mind is in there many time. If I can't go, I feel upset about it, might get sick. If you live in another place too long, you get homesick—a lot of people get homesick for their country.

If you go every now and then you feel good, you got the feeling of it, feeling of the land itself, comes from being on the land. The land gives you something to think about. Life can be harder too, if you find nothing there on the land, no food or water. It is good to have somebody with you. It's all right if lots of people go. By yourself you may feel lost there, nobody left to go with you who knows the country. Some Aboriginal people like me were grown up away from their country like in a mission or settlement. If you know the country you don't need anybody. But you do think a lot if you are there by yourself. When no one is there, you get that feeling that you can talk to the land and the land can talk to you— it come into your mind if you're on the land itself. You can think about the country more better when you're there, in it.

If they dam the Fitzroy River, many people lose all that and they can't ever get it back. The government have to give them compo, but land is more important than money. Money doesn't stay with you, you only have it and the next day it might be gone. The land will always be there, it never go away, when we die it will still be there. It all depends if the people want to fight for money or the land. One old man said, 'I sooner have the land, not the money.' I think that, too.

When people know nothing, that's when they get cheated

Many Aboriginal communities are having lot of problems getting proper administration and making progress. They don't seem to be able to get up for long time. In many communities, people still today only have basic things like clinic, school, office and one shop, but not much else. No money to build up places for people to do their art and sell it, a community meeting place, swimming pool, place for the young teenagers to get together or train for something, nothing. Mostly their houses are not really good either.

Many community people don't know much about how to get funding for things and how to put it on paper. They can't understand these things 'cause nobody explain and show them. One case I know where people did try to get funding; they didn't get treated right. That happen in Kalumburu; my brother-in-law want to apply for funding for his tourism business and he talk to ATSIC. Bloke came out from some Business Enterprise Centre to help him and fill out papers. Later, in about one year, he bin told he'd get money for new building, a toilet block with showers, and a vehicle. After two years gone, he was still waiting. We investigated and after long time and many, many phone calls, we find that funding application never got past the first stage. Nobody bin doing any more on it. It was sitting there in some office and the people in the community wait to go to collect their new four-wheel-drive vehicle, bin told money come for building any day now.

These days community elect a council to look after things in the place. Council is Aboriginal, but still white people do the administration of the community in many cases. Sometime this goes well, many places it's not too good, 'cause some of the white people are no good. Also council can have big problems in their job 'cause they all can be related to people in the community and even to one another on the council. There are problems some other non-Aboriginal people don't understand, and I like to explain some of those things.

Now when the mission is no longer there, people should be able to support themselves and organise the community better. Problem is some are too used to thinking they can't get up by themselves. One trouble is money. People can't handle money well yet in some places, especially if they been under mission rule. Where it was a mission, people never really got used to money. They don't even know what money is to them; it didn't even come in until the middle 1960s in Kalumburu. Aborigines there, they got no idea of handling money before.

It's very hard to deal with the problem when people in the community never bin in charge of their own money. When the money come in from the government, it was handled by the mission. Now this time in some communities, there's certain change, this time they got a shop in the community, not run by the mission. But I know these days in some communities, shop is still looking after the money for the pensioners. Instead of money going to the mission, it goes to the shop now, which is handled by the white shopkeepers in most cases, as far as I know. I know pensioners that, still today, got no idea about pension money belong to them, like how much they have. Many of these shops are still not run by Aboriginal people. I think only as people run their own facilities can they have control of it. When you know nothing, that's when you get cheated.

Right now, many remote Aboriginal people still cannot handle money. They don't really know how to keep books, don't know how to keep the account, keep ordering things people want to buy, how to pay tax, they not trained for these things. Some younger people know now how to handle money, but mostly spend it too quick and don't use it really well.

Few people that know how to keep books, they prefer to work outside. There are better living conditions in town, better pay. They can do better there than live in the community, because they got lot of problems in the community. Outside, in the town, they don't have so many people humbugging them all the time. I got experience myself of that. They don't have to put up with relatives humbugging them, 'cause relations sometime cannot look after themselves, so they're more better off living away from the family. Relations often rely on somebody else—long as they know people got money in their pocket, they ask to share. That should be stopped.

Old pensioners in communities, especially if they get cash on pension day, they might have it for one day, but other people, they think it's a good thing to give money away. People enjoy that, someone else's money. If you look at it 'nother way, that make you mad, cause that is your money; you the one that work for it long hours while other people did exactly nothing.

Even when old people sleep, 'nother person might come in the house, take food and money or radio or anything, I seen it happen. Or when someone's drunk they come and take things. In the olden days, nobody wasn't allowed to steal anything from other people. This come in only lately. All our traditional rules died off, never bin passed to the younger people, 'cause they bin put in the dormitory and they didn't like the white rules. That mean really now they have no rules at all.

For some people it's easy to ask for money. People did that lots of times to me—many people ask me for money. Straight away my feelings no good. I don't ask others for money, or if I borrow it, I give it back to them. Mostly people never pay you back. Some people say, 'Oh, you have money all the time.' I say to them, 'How you know that? I'm a blackfella like you; I'm not a white man. I work for money. If I can save money, you can save money too.' Lot of people ask me like that. Some people think to get money is easy, but they reckon it's not that easy to save money. I know that, like, when they get money they go out and gamble or drink. I just tell 'em if I can save, you can do that too.

Trouble is, you can't tell 'em anything because it's too far gone with some. I try, I tell the young ones, 'Don't spend money on drink or smoke. If you got nothing, too bad, you don't go asking people, them days are gone for asking, nobody doesn't give money to people. What happen if I had nothing? Nobody give me anything, easy as that.'

Long time ago when people used to share things, it was mostly food. Someone kill kangaroo, people don't go ask the bloke who kill it for anything. He's in charge of doing things, might be he has to feed his relation, cousins. He is the one who share it out, 'nother people just wait for him, they don't go and ask, they sit down and wait. This fella, his job is to give to certain people only and what is left is for him. Don't give any people anything. Just like you only give money to others if you share a house or something like that.

'Nother problem is the way people has bin given CDEP* money. CDEP is a same money people get for dole, it is a dole money, but Aborigines have to work to get it. You don't see white people work for the dole. That's not fair for a start, an' a lot of Aboriginal people don't want to work for the CDEP because it's not proper wages, not proper award rates. Maybe that's why people walk off Carson River Station lately.

In the mission people never bin taught going somewhere else to train. Not many of us even knew that other sorts of schools or colleges existed. I never heard of universities 'til I went to Perth much later. Sometime, when Aboriginal people wanted to be educated more, they wasn't allowed to go out of some of the missions. In Kalumburu we only bin taught basic things. Girls were only trained for house work, washing clothes, look after little kids, and the boys for station work, to be stock boys and labourers for work on stations or on the missions, wherever they wanted to go.

Somebody I knew from Forrest River Mission, he wanted to come to Perth to get better education, he thought of it himself. One day the Reverend there said to that young man he could go with him for education down south, the Father even consulted with his

* *Community Development Employment Program*

parents. All agreed that he should go to get better education. He was taken and put on a farm to work as a labourer, unpaid. He was stuck there for three years, all the time waiting to start his new education—it never come. I later work with that man. In Kalumburu one woman wanted to learn to be an air hostess but mission stopped her.

I wanted to become a priest or brother. I wrote to the Bishop down at New Norcia, Abbot Gregory. I wrote to him a letter an' then he wrote to me. I got letter back with a holy picture. I think the Abbot said he will keep my request or something like that. I show that to Father Sanz one day and he said, 'Oh yeah, that's good.' Soon after, one day the Abbot came on a regular visit and he said to me, 'Oh, that place, New Norcia, is no good for you to come, it's too cold for you down there.' Everything was decided for us, nobody ask our opinion. From there I forgot about becoming ordained, and live normal life.

Because people were under mission rules all the time, they didn't learn how to administrate themselves later. It's very hard when you're under rules all the time. When independence come, people wait for the other person all the time to do something. Nobody know how to make rules any more.

In the end, white people come into the community to do the work we can't do. Some white people in the community took off with heaps of money. They stay for a couple of years and then take off, happen in Oombulgurri and in other places. In Oombulgurri not long ago bloke took off with a whole lot of money, but I think he got caught, I remember that one.

Well, I think some of these white administrators; they don't think much of Aboriginal communities. They only want to get money to fill their pocket, and they had no idea about Aboriginal people. I know some call us bad names, layabout bastards, lazy dickheads, arrogant pricks and good for nothing, hopeless—an' that's what they're good for, these people only like the money. They live in the best house in the community, they suppose to help the council organise things, but nothing much moves. I know of one case, where a woman administrator was attacked by community women for making rules they didn't like. In many communities, white people still run all essential things like school, clinic, shop, and office. Even the petrol is still sold by the church in Kalumburu to this very day.

White people like that got long way to go, if they think they can educate Aboriginal people to be like white people. Better for Aboriginal people to do things the way we see it best, then it can work. Oombulgurri is a small community, the other side of Wyndham. People there finally got a good, strong council and strong Aboriginal leaders an' they do really well now. Lot of trouble before, after mission left in 1968. They all moved to Wyndham, then they saw what it's like to live in a town, people getting in trouble, into drink and jail; that's why they turn around, and move back again. They didn't like the town, they now prefer to look after their own community.

White people in my days had a lot of power and experience too. People in remote area, they only live in the bush, they don't know much about what white people do to this day. Sometime even a good council can get a hard time. Aboriginal way, we look after our own relation and relationships, that's what counts most with Aboriginal people. It's what kept us alive in the old days. That council system is 'nother white way and I think it don't suit all us Aboriginal people, we might have to find 'nother way to get things done. It just like two things going against each other and people need time to work it out proper way. But I think we best hurry up, or the world might leave us behind. Aboriginal people couldn't find a way to be independent before, because you couldn't do nothing when white people rule over you. Aboriginal people can still see that today and that's why it's very hard to break out of it, to break through. They never learned how to think for themselves. Mission don't allow them. Sometime they're frightened to approach white people. We ask for many things but we also get knocked back many times.

Now we're free an' if we try hard and look at the big picture, we can find new ways and new ideas.

A lot to learn

While I was living in Kalumburu we knew very little about the government or government policies. We all knew the Prime Minister was Mister Menzies, where they stay, where the capital city was. In the mission school, they said Prime Minister is the one that rule the country. They live in the Parliament House, they rule there, and they told us who is the government for each state. Outside Kalumburu we only knew of Welfare and how they control people in the town reserve and elsewhere outside. We really only knew missionaries, Welfare, doctor and the police, that's all. We knew very little about places like Darwin, Wyndham, Derby, and Broome, too.

We heard of Sydney, Melbourne, Brisbane and others as we used to have a map hanging in the school. Like they said, we live in Western Australia, next door is Northern Territory. They tell us where the border line is on the map, that's how much we know, but we had no idea how people are controlled outside, none of us knew, Kalumburu was just in a little corner. I think in those days, we believe that people everywhere have someone to control 'em, like we were under the control of the mission. They told us about Queensland in the mission school and other states, but I don't know what it's like to live there in those places. We only knew the mission and we heard of other missions like Beagle Bay and Forrest River Mission.

Old Mary told us how she and Manuela Puruan went to school there at Beagle Bay. When they were young, she said, they were taken on the State Ship *Koolinda*, just taken and put on the ship at Kalumburu. Mary Pandilo had parents and she told us not long ago how sad she was cause she thought she'd never see her mother again. Mission sent the two girls to school in Beagle Bay, and they came back many years later.

From the Sisters in school we hear a lot about outside, but have no idea what it's like to stay there, so I thought one day I find out.

It was only when I left Kalumburu and work on the stations that I find out more about Aboriginal way of living. Because the Aboriginal people were free outside in the stations where they work, they were free to follow their Aboriginal ways. Even people in Kalumburu who live in the outside camps, away from the mission compound, used to stick to their own culture much as they could. You saw people dancing there, but in the mission we couldn't do that. We mission children were separated from our people or family, and from our own Aboriginal ways. Nobody tell us about 'em in the mission, and I think our old people didn't teach us about our culture because we were in the mission.

When I look back now, I see that we didn't even realise what we missed out on—only much later I find that the white people took our culture away from us and that I am poor in my Aboriginal ways because of that. The white ways we bin taught in the mission don't make up for what is lost. You can't do a change just like that.

The Mirriwung and Gajerrong are the people that belong in the Kununurra region all around. I learn from them in the station, they were good people, very nice people and I learn a lot from them after I left the mission. Aboriginal people say more there, 'bout things that concern them, their own business. In the mission they don't say anything much like that; outside they talk about all these things.

I never learn much about our rights, like human rights and legal rights. Only in the 1970s, I heard about that. I don't believe Aboriginal people had any rights in those days, come to think of it. We only knew Welfare sometime look after Aboriginal people; later on it was Aboriginal Affairs. I only heard of it when they got strike in Wave Hill Station near Katherine, Northern Territory, in the '60s. I was thinking how they did that, want more wages and go on strike. We all heard of it and didn't know what that was for exactly, and how they all walk off. It wasn't 'til long time after that, when I heard that Aboriginal people bin on strike already in the Pilbara in the early 1940s with Don McCleod, who bin help Aboriginal people there.

Wave Hill was a big company. Lord Vestey, he owned that. I heard the news first when Mrs Peters, manager wife on Argyle Station, she told me. I was mowing the lawn then, she came out and told me the Aboriginal people walk off at Wave Hill. I said, 'What for?' She told me they are fighting for award wages. I didn't even know what that was. The owner said that was too much and there won't be any work on the station for that sort of pay. I said to the missus I know nothing about it. She told the Aboriginal working girls there too. She heard it on the radio, no labour left on the station at Wave Hill. I ask, 'Did they argue or what?' She said, 'No, they only want more money.'

From there, was nothing. Nobody thought about it any more, they didn't follow it up, people was happy on Argyle station; we just listen to news what is happening next with them, the strikers. Later when I was in Kununurra, I hear bit more. No television in those days. Station had newspaper, Western Mail come from Darwin. In Wyndham I start reading newspaper, The West Australian paper.

First I don't understand much in the paper, but I learn little by little by asking people. I read about things slowly. I heard about the tent embassy some Aboriginal people set up in Canberra, but had no idea what it was. First time I went to Canberra was much later. When we live in Kalumburu in 1996, Traudl and I got invited to a workshop for Aboriginal oral history. The Australian Institute for Aboriginal and Torres Strait Islander Studies in Canberra paid for us to go 'cause we did recordings with people in Kalumburu then. I thought Canberra would be a much interesting place to see as it is the capital city where the parliament is, and the Opposition and the Senate, and where the rules and power comes out from. It was the first time I travel that far and I very much enjoyed everything.

It was very interesting for me to see the new Parliament House and the old one. That one remind me of the Whitlam Government that was in power once. I like the Whitlam government. It was good for Aboriginal people because that was the time when the government start to give land back to our people.

Down the other side, there was still the Tent Embassy, and I saw the big High Court building. That's where the Land Rights and Mabo legislation come out, and that's a very good thing. I also saw the big Australian National University and they gave us a flat in there; everything was really good, including the workshop.

I started to learn about politics when I was out of the mission, about the Opposition, the Senate and the Upper and Lower Houses. You are independent outside, and slowly, little by little, I learn, first on the station, then in town like Wyndham. Later I work in Geraldton, even in Perth, and then I work in Kununurra for long time, later in Derby, and Port Hedland. In Hedland, I did a course in horticulture and then I got a job there as well. I see newspapers and television, and I go to movies. First time I hear what's happening in the outside world. When I can't understand, I used to go and ask some people that know more. I ask 'em anything and they tell me, that's how I learn. I wasn't interested in politics much. I don't like what I don't know. Only later, I think maybe if I know more about it, politics might be good for something.

Politics was no good for people like me, even if I know more, I think I won't like it. People mostly don't understand politics, it might lead to something like trouble, I see that all the time. Nobody I know ever talk about politics 'til later on. If you can follow it, might be it's good to get on in the government. Ernie Bridge was the only Aboriginal politician in WA for a long time and now it's Carol Martin for that seat—still the only one. There should be more, but Aboriginal people still have too much trouble on the ground, no time to think high about politics. Our people mostly don't get good education for big things like that. Well, I just thought it's a good thing to be an Aboriginal person in the politics. Ernie Bridge might have more ideas about things others don't know, because they don't know the country like he does. He lived in the bush; other politicians don't grow up as he did.

Now, these days, people can ask for what they need or want. Before we only had one Australian flag, which is mostly the English flag. Now I'm glad we got Aboriginal flag, which is really good thing. The Australian flag stands for the people who brought the flag here, but Aboriginal people was here before, living in this country. The Aboriginal flag is very important, that stand for us the Indigenous people, it stands for the country and the people in it—make me feel good when I see the colours. Now you see sometime people carry that flag with them in the street for demonstration and rallies, and Cathy Freeman did well when she carried our flag.

Other good thing bin happen is Reconciliation. That's for people coming together for better understanding. Too many people don't even know a single Aboriginal person, especially in the city, I think. When I'm in Perth city, I see some people look at me like they never seen Aboriginal people before. Some are children. Don't know whether parents teach 'em that Aboriginal people are indigenous people from this land. When I walk in the street, I see children stare at me just like they haven't seen anyone like me before. Up in the north in the Pilbara and Kimberley children don't do that because they know 'bout Aboriginal people. They see Aboriginal children in the school and play with them. Even I don't see many of my people down here in the city, and I miss seeing them. Up north they're everywhere and I feel good having them around.

One day in 1997, when I was in Perth, we went for a walk in the bush behind Jarrahdale in the forest along a creek. Two teenage girls were playing in the creek when I walk towards them from under the trees. When they saw me suddenly come out from the bush, they got the fright of their life and they quickly run away. I know they were scared of me, because I see their face change like they saw a ghost, and they spin around and run out of the creek on the other side. I think they never seen an Aboriginal person like me before.

'Nother good thing is Aborigines know more about their rights now. Long time ago no Aboriginal people anywhere demonstrate about anything, they couldn't do that. Now they demonstrate because they know more, and they're able to stand up for themselves and for what we want.

I don't think we have enough Aboriginal leaders to help us and discuss things with us and talk to the government. We need some Aboriginal people to be in power with the government to have a say in what's happening in the country. We need more Aboriginal people doing politics because they understand their own people and they could talk for us.

Ambrose and Laurie Waina (Ambrose's father's cousin brother), repairing a plough, Kalumburu

Hunting at Oomari, 1998

Ambrose sitting on the plough years later (We root the snakes out with the plough)

In the Bungle Bungles (Purnululu), 1997

Clearing rocks to build a road
(L to R: Murrel, Francis Waina, Ambrose, Old Placid)

Br John Richards and Ambrose in the pineapple crop

Kwini tales from the Dreamtime

Oonggoorr and other snakes

There are lot of snakes in the Kimberley. During the winter time, when it's cooler weather they walk around, well, they walk around when it's dry season. Cooler weather start end of April; then in May, June, July, people travel in the bush like we do.

Snake mostly only go for you if they have friends, and they're mating. If you go near them, or if he got nest, you know that's the only time they go for you. Wherever we camp in the bush, we lay a rope right around, because we don't believe that snake goes over the rope. I don't know where I got it from; most people in the Kimberley I know believe it. I think it comes from ringers, they always carry rope, white and Aboriginal, they all mixed. People think snake don't like going over a rope.

Snakes move around, they hunt mostly during the day. You don't see them just because you want to see them; you notice them along the river or anywhere. When they hear you come, they leave you alone; when they hear a sound, they go 'nother way, see, but if you don't make noise you see them near.

Either they get a fright or you do—for sure I do. Only thing, they bite if you got 'em in a corner or tread on them by accident. Then they feel threatened, they strike quick, too, or if you try to kill 'em. Like one day when I was working, I spray the weed Noogoora Burr along the Ord with APB and I don't know how, but I didn't see the snake. I walk right past it and 'nother fella came and sing out, 'Oh, snake here!' I said, 'I musta bin walk right past it.'

There was one young white bloke who said, 'I'll kill it.' I told 'im 'No', but he said, 'I'll kill it,' so I turn around and watch what he was going to do. The snake lay very still now, didn't move anywhere; the man hit 'im with a stick and snake jumped very quick, nearly got 'im and almost bite 'im on the thigh. After he walk away in a fright. Later he never eat anything. I turn around ask 'im, 'Anything wrong with you?' he said, 'Yeah, by golly, I nearly got bitten.'

From there I explain it to him; if you kill a snake, you hit 'im while he's moving, but not when he's still, that's the worst thing, because he can strike you easily. I said, 'We're a long way to the doctor.' We didn't even have a two-way radio when we work with APB in 1982-83. Argyle Diamond Mine was there but it was far away, or Lissadell Station, but by the time we run there, you could be dead. Later when the new type of vehicle came in, they had proper radios, but for many years we had nothing. I work with them from 1979; somewhere around 1985 we had radio for first time. Before we only have radio in the truck for music. Sometime when people get sick, they used to take 'em to hospital in the truck.

Sometime snake comes looking for warm place to sleep in the night. One day my brother told me they bin camping in the bush in Oombulgurri there, one man got up and the snake came out of the swag after he had got up, a king brown. It bin sleeping with 'im. The fella looked to see if he bin bitten, but he was all right.

Snakes like warmth; they curl up where it's warm. In Kalumburu, we had one in the middle of our swag, three times. One thing that bring snake to a camp, they like music. I seen it lot of time. I had little radio on, too, and later I walk out for toilet, I see snake curled up, resting. They hear music long way. Only thing you got 'im beat, when you shine a torch in his eye he can't see, you blind him, he move very slowly then.

In the old days, Aboriginal people had the dogs, they didn't need any rope, or lasso, the dogs bark when they smell or hear something. Aboriginal people didn't have to do anything; dogs are the most helpful. There are all kinds of snakes in the Kimberley you come across. 'Nother one is the tree snake, the yellow one. That snake move faster in the tree than on the ground. The tree snake when they move, they got their heads up like that, not like the ground snake, it go flat. I don't like tree snake because it eats eggs in the birds' nest. Python does that, too.

One night I stop on the road, it was a python; I just stopped to have look. I grab hold of him and look at him; it was just about sunset time. I got hold of it because I was a bit drunk. I don't kill anything unless some time you can't help it. You can't touch king brown. Snake catcher, they got special thing to capture them like that, but some people get it when it's moving. I seen a bloke hold it like a whip by the tail. Python sometime they come to your house too. They can climb up if you have a chook yard, they like that, and they smell milk sometime. A python climb up roof too, sometime they climb up to get bird; they eat 'em. One time I see one swallow big duck, I seen it along the water just walking along. Next thing it was in the python. I got closer and closer and its belly was big, swollen. It look like it swallowed a ball. I walk past 'im and he was so fat he doesn't move.

Some people say taipan bin seen in the Kimberley. I only know king brown, tree snake, death adder, wala (whip snake), that one go fast too, they can bite. You can get swollen too, but they're quiet, not poisonous. They can be aggressive.

That Rainbow Snake, the Oonggoorr, Dreamtime Snake, only little I know about that. They reckon Rainbow Snake bring luck. It bring rain, it lives in the water and sometime it form into something like a spirit so that it becomes the rainbow. Long time ago it also form mountains and valleys. If you kill that snake, water will go dry. I think I believe that because of what happened one day at Winanghie. We were all there, Francis Waina, me, other boys and all the nuns; the same place where I show you.

We bin fishing there on the beach, yeah, and somebody saw a snake going down the spring water, the same water we use for boiling the billy. That fresh water spring was back from the beach, a bit, in the bush. I showed you the waterhole, there used to be a lot of water there. In that spot there when we were coming back from fishing, there was a water snake. It was pretty long, just like a python, big, it took us a long time to get it. We was trying to get it out, we got it by the tail and pull it little by little, it was that hard, it took a long time to get it out. It was a water snake, and we killed it.

We didn't know we not supposed to do that. It was the water snake, it belong to the water all the time.

We just thought of killing it there because we were frightened of it, we kill it with a stick. Nuns took a picture with a camera; they show us the photo when we were eating in the dining room some time later.

Later on we realised we shouldn't kill it; we didn't think of anything in those days. That time we didn't have any old people with us, or they would've told us what to do. I was about twelve or thirteen. I think that time Francis Waina just came back from leprosarium. From dormitory we used to go every Sunday for picnic. We only go to the spring to get fresh water for the billy; we was only interested in fishing. After we bin back one week later, we saw water was very low then, only that much left. Right to the top, it bin full but when we went back it had gone right down, and from there it was nothing, we had to go and get water a little bit further.

We said, 'Ah, because we killed the snake, the water went down, might be snake was the one to keep the water.' We realise snake must be the keeper of that permanent water. You change your understanding when you see things; we only realised that when the thing happened. Before we didn't think we'd done something wrong.

When you brought up in the mission it's different, you don't have your parents. In the bush all the time you among everything. It's different in the bush, in the bush we could have bin different, we could've know all about well, snakes, and the bush and the dream time stories. In the dormitory you are under instruction when you go to sleep, when you get up, when you have your meals, all that thing. Part of it we didn't care because we had meals there; that was the main thing. Long as you eat in that place, you're all right.

When you think about it now you look at the big picture. I can say now it wasn't good to kill that snake, but we just didn't know. We had to find out 'bout our culture later.

animal yarns

How Micky cheated the crocodile

This is a story about a man and a crocodile and it happened at Drysdale River.

The people were on walkabout when one old man called Micky, he swim in the Drysdale River near to the mouth, where there's a lot of *meniwurra* (flying fox). Meniwurra is good to eat. Old Micky was related to me, he was Kwini, too. His family was from Oombulgurri.

Micky climb up a tree to kill the flying fox. He had a stick in his hand—nobody handled a gun in those days. He got up the tree and killed some meniwurra but a few fell in the river. So when he saw two or three fall in the water, he jump down and rushed into the water to get 'em. People in the Kimberley know almost every river has crocodiles, but some time they think they might be lucky. Now, just as Micky was swimming, the croc suddenly came from underneath the water and took 'im.

He was young man then. Long time later I could still see the scars and big marks in his back from the crocodile. Croc got hold of him, pull 'im down with his teeth. He took 'im underneath in the middle round his waist; he hold 'im in his jaws. Lucky the old man was clever. He thought the more he struggle, the more he hold you, so this fella didn't move, pretend he was dead already. Croc pull 'im down in a cave under the sandbar, and left 'im there. He put 'im there, you see, that's what crocodile do, when they let big meat get rotten, then they eat it. They do that to the cattle too; they mostly don't eat meat fresh.

Micky was acting dead, so croc went away. Soon as he knew croc was gone, he slide down, stir up the mud, swim away and manage to get out. Bit later croc came back to look for him. He float around, look everywhere for him, but Micky was on the bank already. He said, 'See you,' and walked back to his camp. He was bleeding and when the people saw him, they cried and said, 'We thought you are dead!' Well, they all bin there, they saw the croc take 'im and pull 'im under, and they left and cried when he didn't come back up.

Now they look at him, they make him sleep and put special medicine on him, so that blood won't come out any more. They burned special plant and when it was still hot they put it on the wound. They kept him there for long time. It healed up, but when I was young he still had croc mark on his back, all around, and I seen it. He was still working again for many years afterwards, and he used to go walkabout 'round Lullbay, Londonderry, and Drysdale River.

Jun-goo and the big kangaroo

There was Jun-goo, Augustin and Dangall all gone hunting one day along Paradise Pool and Pundia Creek. Nowadays people hunt with guns. In those days, they go with a spear. They used to get ant pads from termite mounds, break it up and rub it on their body so kangaroo won't smell you come. The ant pads have a special smell, like a modern deodorant people use now. Except you couldn't use that for hunting 'cause kangaroos don't know that new smell and they still run away. Ant pad they know and they don't think it's a man coming, see. Ant pad has a smell like the ground when it bin raining. You can use bit of mud too, anything like that will do. People sneak up on the kangaroo without making a sound. Sometime they make a small circle of fire. They leave a gap for the 'roo to come out and when it runs out they spear it. The kangaroos can't see the people through the smoke.

Anyway, that day between there and Carson River, the men speared this huge kangaroo. Old man Jun–goo spear it and it run off with the spear stuck inside him. Half way the spear broke, but the kangaroo kept running away and the dog chase it. The kangaroo run into a waterhole to get away from the dog, but the dog follow him. In the water, the 'roo turn around and grab the dog, and with his two claws hold 'im down under the water and try drown him in the middle of the creek.

Old man Jun-goo rush to save his dog just in time. He managed to get his spear out but the 'roo grabbed him. He hit the kangaroo with a stick. It let the dog go and got hold of the man instead now and pull him down, too. They were wrestling, struggling together. The man tried to come out, but the 'roo want to drown him. Old man couldn't win 'cause the kangaroo was very strong and pretty big and the man realised he had to do something quick. He went under between the kangaroo's legs and bit him on the nuts—and that's how the kangaroo finally let go of him after all.

He got out of the water and the three men decided, 'We better leave this one alone,' and run off. Because the kangaroo was so big and strong and clever, they thought it might be some sort of a ghost or spirit.

People know the kangaroos in that place are really big, nearly as tall as a person, and old man Jun-goo was a bit short. A man alone can't even carry a 'roo that big, we have to take turns, they're that heavy. We did that once, we change over. In the old days people had a special way to make the young men strong: carry a kangaroo over their shoulder long way over rocks and barefoot. Our men used to be strong and tough then.

Wild cattle bin spread everywhere

Long time ago as I bin brought up in the mission, every one of us in the dormitory including me, we never seen a bull or cattle, 'til I was about twelve years old. We had no idea what cattle look like. We thought it was big as a horse. Mainly nanny goats we see and pigs and horses and donkeys. I think missionaries brought donkeys to the Kimberley. Later, we used to have donkeys too for riding; we brought 'em out of the bush to quieten 'em down in the mission.

All the time then, we see only dead bull, pieces of bull, really. Our men from the mission used to go to Pago (about 29 km north of Kalumburu) to get some meat—we call it 'get a killer'. There was no cattle in Kalumburu area yet. Pago had cattle already some time ago, because it was where Kalumburu Mission first set up before it moved to where it is now. I think they drove cattle from Forrest River area to Pago. Some Aboriginal men were sent out by mission to bring back salted meat, and that was the only time we saw the horns. We thought that must be a very big animal. Horse used to bring everything, all the meat in big hessian bags, pocket hanging down with salt meat both sides, even the bones. Meat was salted on the spot where they kill it and they bring it in small chunks, every bit of it the horse brought back.

When Father Basil became superior he thought of getting cattle from Gibb River Station. He used to get in touch with Fred Russ, manager at Gibb River. There was no telephone in those days, only radio message. The men went in wintertime. They pack up in Kalumburu. They're all dead now, the men, only Basil left. Old Jun-goo went with them, one that got attacked by kangaroo once.

It was around 1952. They take a spare horse to change for riding and carrying things. Road wasn't build in those days yet. It was old Jun-goo who knew the way, 'cause the old Aboriginal people used to walk up and down all the time so they knew the way. After a good while, we heard they had reached Gibb River. The track used to go all along past Carson River Station. Jack Eggleston had it then, he came from Ireland. The old road goes through that jump-up, Miljenki it's called. I think it's Walmbi language—where that fence line is, the old road go through the big hill there. The boys stay there for two or three weeks and then we heard they had left with five or six hundred cattle. Mission bought it from Fred Russ. Cattle used to be pretty cheap in those days, but I don't know how much it cost. Basil, his brother Wagan, Robert, Augustin and Joseph, I think, all went. Joseph is a Kwini; the others were Kulari and Walmbi. Joseph and Jun-goo died long time ago. The old men knew cattle from before, they seen cattle at Pago and knew how to handle cattle from there. Father Basil himself went, too, he was pretty young then, and he was a horse rider.

Then we heard they were coming back to Kalumburu with the cattle. They had lot of trouble half way, bit of trouble from wild bulls when they come up. Bull come and stir up the mob, yeah, they had trouble with the cattle. It was no station around there, only Gibb River. Places like Kunmunya, Port George Mission, and Kingana they all had cattle and they had spread out. Later, all that cattle there was wild. That's where the scrub bulls come from.

They come in and fight with the others in the mob on the way to Kalumburu, and cause trouble. In those days they had no yard with 'em. People had to take it in turn to walk around on a horse all night. Cattle are there in one place and people had to walk around. That's the danger, when they get frightened they can rush and people have to look for tree because they'll run over anything. Happened in one place, cattle bin rushed and people, when they were sleeping, they had to jump up and scramble behind trees at a place called Talngga. Drysdale River Station wasn't there then, and that's what the place was called before white man name.

And then when they were finally coming, the men and the cattle stopped for two weeks at Moormoor, Paradise Pool, not far from Kalumburu. From there, Father Basil went to the mission alone to tell 'em they're coming. When you come back with cattle it's very slow. They move slow, not like horses. I think it took them two months to bring the cattle from Gibb River, maybe 300 km away. Father Basil went into the mission to warn 'em, 'Cattle will be here in the afternoon, there must be no noise, no barking of dogs, the church bell must not ring, all must be quiet.'

There was no cattle yard yet in Kalumburu; they had to come into the big paddock where the mango trees are now, near where the old Kwini camp was. Near Laoar Creek there was a big gate and cattle come through there, through Tingun Paddock, that's where the old track come through. You know, the Cemetery Creek in Tingun where we cross over, that's the place. When the cattle was coming closer, we all went out in the paddock, but made no noise. All the boys and girls and Brother came to look. First we saw nothing, could only hear the cracking of the whip and then we saw clouds of dust. We never saw cattle, and now we could hear the noise, the mooooh sound. Then we saw one rider was leading in the front and all the cattle must follow him and stay in a group all the time. It was afternoon then and behind the front rider, we could now see them—crack! went the whip and crack! again—we were sitting on top of the mission fence and they're coming closer—now we can see what cattle look like at last, we were very excited.

You know where the garage is now, that's where they stopped. There was a fence all around. They left 'em there for the night, inside the fence. Brother said 'They're used to people and being in a yard.'

We were so happy to see them. We liked the cattle and got closer to have good look. Some were pretty quiet. Brother told us, 'You cannot touch 'em, some might not be quiet and they have horns, they can horn you and be very dangerous sometimes.' For long time we used to be satisfied to walk past them.

Soon they had few calves. First time we saw calf, we used to like 'em, night-time they're born, and Brother told us not to touch the calves. He said mother might chase us and we were just happy to look. Later, when they kill some cattle, they used to do it when they take the cattle out for water. They kill one shooting from the horse. Horse not frightened, they used to .303. Horse know the noise from the gun, they can handle it, and people shoot from the side. 'Nother way they used to climb up in a tree on top and shoot from there, only once a week might be. Later on, they brought special bulls from Fossil Downs, that's from Tableland area— Yulmbu it's called.

From there every day we see the cattle, they used to stay all around Laoar Creek. Barton Plain Station at Jiliwei, they were building it up with cattle when they got more. Regi Tie, white man was there. From time they went to get cattle, Jiliwei belong to the mission, Lesley French used to work there. That's where he got burned and my brother-in-law saved him by riding all night to get help. Mission had a lease there; it was a house, a windmill and a tank, the one that Lesley took later to use at Honeymoon Beach. I don't know what went wrong there at Barton Plain. The place was abandoned after.

Later the mission got more cattle. Frank Lacey brought some from Gibb River Station, later, with his son, Peter, and his own horses. Mission paid him to bring the cattle, four or five hundred head. From there, more bulls came, three or four on a ship from Derby. They brought them, different kind with no horns, name Santa Gertruda, all from Fossil Down Station. A ship took the bulls there from Derby to a spot near Sir Graham Moore Island, then waited for the lugger to get 'em. The mission lugger load 'em up out at sea and take 'em to Longhani near Kalumburu.

Father Basil went to Longhani, that's the landing place, then. The lugger had a steel floater, big pontoon; they got that from Truscott airbase. The pontoon had big pipes to hold the cattle, like a pen, and the lugger pulled it behind. It was used for heavy stuff, towed by the lugger, half of the cargo used to go on the pontoon.

It was solid, made out of steel, flat, fitted with timber on the floor for the cattle to walk. Truck could fit on it, two trucks; it was pretty long. At Longhanie bulls walk out on a plank when the tide was high, and the pontoon floated up level with the land. Stock boys were waiting to pick 'em up. The bulls were quiet ones.

Scrub bulls are not like that; they can be very fierce. One day something happened with one of them: Wagan, Augustin, Leo, and Robert were send all out to get meat before they brought cattle from Gibb River. Bull meat was tough, but people didn't mind. They had a spare horse and went to South Creek on the way to Pago, where we swim that time, you and me. First they couldn't find anything. Then they come on to a very big bull. Someone shot 'im but only wounded 'im, so bull ran away. He had spit coming out of his mouth, he was really wounded and he went long way. Well, cane grass was very high, too, not green, all dried out. Augustin said, 'I follow him,' and went front to see how far the bull went. He had no gun with him.

Augustin went slowly with the horse. When you follow you look on the ground all the time. The bull lay down facing the way he'd come to watch what's coming behind, very clever they are, and Augustin didn't see him yet. Horse knew something was there and just then, all of a sudden bull got up and went for them, knock 'em both down. Augustin had no chance to take off; the bull horned the horse, lift him up and Augustin fall off the horse. Then the bull went straight for Augustin when he wanted to get up. Good luck he quickly went to lie down again flat, so the bull only could rip his trousers and then took off. When a person lies flat he can still reach you with a horn and he can stamp on you.

The horse had blood come out, and when the bull came back again, Augustin went behind a tree. After that, the boys came with the horses and Augustin told 'em what happened. They had to cut his trousers right around. The horse couldn't get up, had blood pouring out and they had to shoot it. Then they looked for the bull and they found him laying down, but when he tried to get up again they shot him and that was the end of that bull.

Wild bulls can worry you when you're camping or walking through bush. Proper wild bull; they never seen a person. If you have dog with you, that's all right, but if you haven't, the bull can destroy your camp. You never know what's in their mind. All of a sudden they can go for you when they see you. You look at them and at that very moment their mind can change very quick. You don't know what he will do from one minute to the next. When you're far away, bull does nothing, but when you come closer he may do something, you just don't know. Snake don't do that, snake only does something if you stamp on him or do something to him, but bulls are not like that.

Once in Wyndham a buffalo chase an old man, but the old man had a dog with him. He was goanna hunting; he had several dogs with him, big ones too. He climb up the tree and the dogs chase the buffalo away. That's why people like to have lots of dogs; they help 'em and protect them.

There's wild cattle all over the place now. That time we went to Oomarri, well, all that cattle we saw bin spread along from Carson River Station area, 'bout 130 km away. When they see that nobody handles them, cattle go further and further away when there's no fence. Some are from Pago and Drysdale River. Cattle go long way when they want to be in a peaceful place. Some cattle could've come from Naran.

Somewhere around Kingana, northwest of Kalumburu, it was a station somewhere not far away. Willie Reid used to live there, and there was someone else there before 'im. We talk about Bob Anderson before, where that old *Mogoo* speared him 'cause he take some Aboriginal women. He was working for somebody on a station there, old Bob Anderson. Aborigines call him *Bobunder*. They couldn't pronounce his name. There was cattle and it breed up there. Doongan and Drysdale River Stations wasn't there, only Gibb River; that was an old pioneer station, a big station and Kalumburu used to buy cattle from them.

Later stations and missions were abandoned. People moved away but left the cattle there, that's why little by little they spread out. These days people take the cattle with 'em 'cause there are road trains now and roads. Before they couldn't. Long time ago the cattle were just left behind.

Pago had cattle see, but when they moved they couldn't take 'em with them, left 'em there, they became wild. Even at Winanghie, cattle from Pago come there, so all these places when you go fishing, you got to beware of wild cattle all the time. Cattle just follow the river, cattle is everywhere, that's what I said at Oomarri, I could just shoot one when we find no food, the rest dingoes can eat, they need food too. At Oomarri recently, cattle come from anywhere. They don't really stay in the hilly area. They live in the sandy, flat area. They only go walkabout in the hills, and they stay near where water is and feed. Animals are like human beings; they need water, too.

Somewhere near Forrest River, before the mission was there, somebody had cattle there, I think. There is a road you can drive all around from Wyndham to Forrest River. Hugo Austla, a kartiya, build that up right around for cattle. His family run that post office in Wyndham, and Hugo, him and one bloke built that road.

When people camp along that track now, they can hear children and people crying—ghosts—people has bin shot there. On the Durack River they bin shot too, we can hear people walk around and cry at night, near to Forrest River. All that is haunted area. People has bin shot there too, all along near the Durack River, by the same people that look for old Lumpia* that time in 1926, police and other white people. I bin told in one of those deep pools there's bones there, human bones. That time I went on a donkey shoot there, that's when people told me.

I didn't go on a droving trip; we could only go where we're told to go in the mission, we didn't ask anything. I work on a horse in Kalumburu. We used to ride to bring the cows in, milking cows. I was scared of the horse, mainly because when I was in the dormitory my brother, he used to make the horse throw me. We used to ride bareback. He frightened the horse behind, so I could fall down. He was older and used to like teasing me. That was his way. He used to come closer and go shoooo! And I fall off twice and got hurt. Horse nearly kicked me, too. I didn't know what happened, the boys told me, and they growl at him for doing it. 'You shouldn't do that,' they said. He did that a few times. I told him, 'Do you want me to die, why do you do that?' But he just laughed. My

*Lumpia speared Frederick Hay, a station developer who raped Lumpia's wife. This initiated the Forrest River massacre, when police sent to investigate, killed a number of Kwini people in reprisal. Lumpia was gaoled. The massacre is disputed by authorities in defiance of persistent local knowledge.

brother used to ride a quiet one; he always gave me the big wild one, so from there I fall down. It didn't stop me from riding though, but I didn't work much with cattle in the mission, only when I left.

Later, when I was working in the bush with the APB we see two bulls fighting one day. The leadin' hand say we stop and have a look. The bulls dig the ground first and kick soil on top to stir 'em up. I think, they chuck the dust over their back with the hooves. I don't know whether it make 'em more wild. I see they were getting stuck into each other, two big Brahman. They were inside a fence line; it had a big strong barb wire. They had a contractor put it up with a machine, and it was pretty new. We pulled up, and watched quietly how they push each other this way and the other way. I saw one bull come close to the fence and it snapped just like a string. A straight, long, strong barb wire that was that thick just snapped in two places when the bull bumped it. They can't feel it much, the Brahman have a very thick skin. And the fence post bends like just that.

The bulls know each other; they understand exactly what they mean when they look at one another. When they get closer after they dig the dust up, they fight one another with the horns; it's a good thing to watch. And they roar with a big noise. 'Nother one might come and stop 'em, a third bull sometime come in between, might be that one joins the fight and 'nother one walk away. They fight over female just like the human beings fight over woman sometime. Animals are the same. It just like you and me saw it when that bloke in Hedland fight over woman, that's why he said to me, 'I better leave town, you never know…'

I think too many cattle damage the bush in the Kimberley. Cattle stamp on the plants, small ones that are supposed to grow, and they get eaten every time they try to grow, and not much is left. Kangaroos don't do that kind of damage on such a large scale. And there's too many big fires each season—I think people should take better care of the bush, not think how they can make money out of it all the time.

working man

Independence from the mission

Independence for the community of Kalumburu started in 1982. I was working in Kununurra Agriculture Department then. Whether the people knew what independence was or whether they like to be independent or not, I'm not so sure. I heard few stories coming out from there. It was then, when they wanted to be independent, that people in the community walk off the mission. Don't know if they all went. They went to Arugun Junction somewhere for meeting. They walk there, the place where King Edward River come in between Carson River and Kalumburu.

They want to be independent from the mission, want to run the community themselves without mission policy. They walk out for very good reason. My brother-in-law was one of the people wanted community be independent. They don't want to be under the mission any more. Mission policy was a bit too strict for them; they wanted to be on their own, without being like prisoners. They bin kept under strict rules there. Like people couldn't go in and out of the mission without permission from the superior.

Once they were outside and they want to come back, they got to ask permission to return. Just like me when I was working outside on a station, I did the same thing. Station manager or the missus speak to the mission on a radio and ask them if I can come to Kalumburu. If people come without permission and arrive in

Kalumburu, they were sent back again. People usually come in on the mail plane once a month. Charter flights was not available in those days. Mission staff always wait at the airstrip for planes, so people couldn't sneak in without mission knowing.

One time, one Kalumburu person come back into Kalumburu and mission sent him back on same flight to Derby 'cause he had no permission. One mission staff went all the way back from the airstrip to the mission and told the superior that a man had come back without permission. Superior told 'im he couldn't stay. The man had paid for his flight in and his family went to meet him at the airstrip. When his wife find out mission won't let him stay, she said, 'We better all leave this place,' and they all left Kalumburu. This man never came back any more.

Some time later another Kalumburu man arrive from Derby on the mail plane. Superior said to him on the airstrip, 'You must go back on this plane,' because he didn't let him know that he's coming. But pilot then turn around and told the superior, 'I am not taking this man back unless you pay me cash right here for his return trip.' Superior did not pay the pilot and the man stayed in Kalumburu.

Even after that, still people kept asking permission from mission to come back to Kalumburu. That only change when the community became independent of the mission rules.

My brother-in-law came to Perth before that for meeting about Kalumburu. Maybe Aboriginal Affairs organised it 'cause all communities were s'posed to be independent then. At that meeting, my brother-in-law said something and later somebody informed the mission. He said something the mission didn't like. I heard that Father Sanz, the superior, did call 'im a rotten apple after that. I didn't know what that means, apple is the one that you eat, but you notice if one go rotten, everything go rotten underneath in the box. Well, my brother-in-law didn't like that and he's the one that help independence come to Kalumburu.

The mission was out in 1985 when I went back there for holiday. That means the mission is still there, buildings and garden and church and brother and nuns and one priest, but it's not running like before. Now people can do whatever they want.

It was a lot different when the mission was there. Oh, people were healthy, they were working, they eat vegetables, they were looked after. When people didn't work they didn't eat. With community independence, everything changed. Aboriginal Affairs or ATSIC put white administrators there. They need administrator because they themselves cannot handle anything. They need somebody to learn 'em how to administrate the office and handle the business. Many people in Kalumburu find that very hard. I think the people supposed to learn something from the administrators and other white people about trade and looking after the community for self-support, but they didn't really learn that.

Like the Mirriwung people in Kununurra, they're different. They're on the outside. They were by themselves all the time but with other people 'round mostly. I know because I live with 'em for long time, and they wasn't in the mission, they work on outside station and later, in town. While they working they're still connected to the land, and that's how they used to stick together, Mirriwung and Gajerrong people together. They learn very quickly because they seen white people take their land and they wanted their land back, they used to talk about it among themselves. They still work for white people, but among themselves, they could do more what they want, no mission made any rules for them.

They live in town where they see everything happen, they not isolated. The people figured out what they themselves want first, and in the end they approached Bob Hannan, a kartiya. He lives there with his Aboriginal wife in Kununurra. He knows two ways, the white man way and the Aboriginal way and he teach 'em properly.

Kalumburu people couldn't do that—they were like in a circle, they only bin looked after by missionaries all the time since they left the bush. I ended up in the mission. We were there all the time, in the mission; we don't know what was outside. Outside was different to what was in the mission, I find out myself after I left. Even now, it's very hard for them; they didn't handle anything very early. Many just have no experience in any sort of management, the people always used to be told all the time, do it this way and that way, so now they have no idea.

On stations, it was different to the mission, too. Aboriginal workers were told what to do mostly by Aboriginal head boy, not white manager. Station manager tell the head stockman what to do for the whole season. The head stockman tell the Aboriginal head boy, who tell the rest of the camp what to do and where to go. Head stockman used to be white in those days, always, and second head boy was Aboriginal. The Aboriginal workers all live in the station reserve, a little way away from the homestead. Morning time, the stock boys all go to the stock quarters and wait for breakfast, and after head stock boy tell Aboriginal people in the bough shed what to do.

We were still told what to do each day like in the mission. The difference was that in the mission, people were told by white missionaries what work to do and how. On stations people were told what to do by Aboriginal head boy. We all work closely with other Aboriginal people—only the head stock boy would tell 'em what to do. We didn't have so much to do with white station manager. 'Nother thing, people also knew the country well where they work, 'cause some of them was born there, too. That make 'em feel good about themselves and the place and work they did. We love the cattle work and we work among the dust. Mostly when people were old enough they were good on a horse and enjoy the work.

They work harder because they work for money. They know what money is and what they can buy with it. In the mission they didn't work as hard as on the station because they didn't get any money or only little bit. They didn't get any pay until the middle of the 1960s. On the station they got more pay than in the mission, we use to get something like £15 a month, but in Kalumburu I used to get only £1 a week for full time work, looking after the pigs and garden work. Station can pay more money because they made money with the cattle.

Money earned on station we used to spend in Wyndham. I myself was there in Wyndham at races time. We all wanted riding boots and trousers and hats, and we went straight to Jimmy Lee Tong's shop. He had a general outfit and tailor shop, and we used to go and buy 'em there. Station people, when they ran out of money, they used to book credit with him for things they want. He gladly did that for them 'cause they would always come and pay him later.

When we went to town, we could buy what we want, we only had that in mind. We see lots of things in the shop and realise we didn't have enough money sometime; that teach us how to save the money for next time.

The Kalumburu people couldn't do that. They didn't know much before independence. In Kalumburu they didn't have no idea of doing what they wanted when the independence came, because they didn't learn anything about looking after themselves before that happens. That's why they are to have somebody from the outside to administrate and tell 'em what should be done and how.

Now this day they still got big problems because of all that. Most administrators who work there just have a good time and good holiday and they fly in and out all the time at community expense. They didn't really care for the community, they didn't teach the people how to run the place themselves. They live in the best house, own the biggest boat. It just like holiday place, they didn't even pay rent, they were earning a big salary and did nothing for us. They didn't improve the place much at all.

My brother-in-law had a vision that he wanted to get up and do something for himself and the community and show to the others what they can do, like encourage the others. Independence brought the people into nothing much yet. Independence means only one thing, they're free, not forced to go here and there, that's the only thing that means a lot. They feel better without mission rules, do whatever they like, if they want to go to the mission or the church, nobody tell 'em where to go or when.

Before people were told to go to church, now they can do what they like, that's the only change, all the rest they battle on their own. They feed themselves, they are happy to do that, and when they want to go to town, they come and go as they please, long as they got money to take 'em. Before they never see what's around 'em, they were not allowed to go unless they ask permission. Also, they had no money to go.

The community set up a council when the mission was still running, but I heard mission first want to run that too. Even now community council still has problems. People still sometimes don't know what they want, they still have very long way to go. Some people get on drugs and get silly in the head, and gamble their money away. But the community did manage to get a nice clinic with one Kalumburu person, Brigid, working there with Sister Lex and the clinic is very good.

WESTERN AUSTRALIA

NATIVES (CITIZENSHIP RIGHTS) REGULATIONS

Form 1

APPLICATION FOR CERTIFICATE OF CITIZENSHIP

I, ... BRIAN SMITH ....
(Full name)

of .... C/o. NATIVE WELFARE, WYNDHAM. W.A. 6740 ....
(Address)

HEREBY APPLY for a Certificate of Citizenship under the Natives (Citizenship Rights) Act, 1944 (as amended).

DATED at ....WYNDHAM.................... this 28TH .... day of ..AUGUST.......... 19 69 ..

....
(Signature of Applicant.)

To the Clerk of Courts

at ....WYNDHAM,........................

RECEIVED this .... 2ᴺᴰ .... day of ...Sept 19 69

N.B.—This application must be accompanied by a Statutory Declaration (Form 2) and a photographic likeness of the applicant, in duplicate, unmounted, size 2½ in. x 2 in., showing head and shoulders.

57493/3/62-5M-O/D.

Ambrose's brother applies to be recognised as a citizen of Australia—
see page 208 for outcome

First time I work for money

Everybody should know people have been fed on a spoon before by the mission in Kalumburu. Nobody went hungry. We were all fed there. That was long time ago. Now people should turn around and work for their own living just like I did. I always work to feed myself and I work hard all the time and all over the place. People need to work to show an example to the young ones who come later.

We didn't bother about not having money in Kalumburu, because everything was free while we stay in the dormitory. I still live in the dormitory for a while, when I got back from holiday. Father sent me out because mission paid my fare. I only went for holiday to Wyndham, one month and a half—Father Sanz time—mission paid for me. I wanted to see what the place was like, went to Wyndham just to look what outside world is like. I was there before once in the hospital, when I was younger. Kununurra wasn't up yet. I wanted to go earlier, but Father Sanz said, 'I send you when you're over 17.' Now I was flown there, one month or two I could stay, but I wanted to come back for Christmas.

I knew where to go in Wyndham. I went to look around. Father Sanz gave me the letter, a cheque I think. He said, 'Give this to Father Carl'. He was the first priest in Wyndham. In a shop, I saw Father Carl and gave him the letter. He said, 'Oh, I saw you in Kalumburu, whenever you want the money, let me know.' Money was for me, spending money. Maybe the cheque was £25.

There was a man called Meehan who used to work for MacRobertson Miller Airline (MMA) or Mickey Mouse Airline, we called it. It was owned by the chocolate people in Melbourne and the family of Captain Horrie Miller. Meehan was the airport man and he used to drive a bus. He also used to work in the office. He's the one knows what people go in and out of town. He used to pick us up from the airstrip. He wore shoes and white socks, a uniform. The air terminal used to be big too. It had a mess, people used to eat there, and fly to Darwin, Perth, and Broome. He drove me to town. He asked me how long I was staying, and said I could book to go back to the airstrip with him later.

That was in early '60s in Wyndham. First time I work for real money ever. To earn a few shillings, I collect empty bottles to sell 'em to the cool drink factory that used to be owned by Les Wild. The bottle had mark on it "Cambridge Aerated Water, Wyndham". People used to sell 'em box full and we could get five shillings, ten shillings out of it, even £1 for selling two or three bags full. That's how one time I earn money middle of the week 'til I had 'nother job. No Social Security in those days, you have to get money to feed yourself.

I go alone when I look for bottles outside the pictures, near the shop along the road, and around movie theatre show. It was only one shop there, the Three Mile Shop, that used to be Ord River Traders before Joe Weir had it, the first shop I saw in the 1960s. 'Nother one was Chinese shop, General Store it was called, opposite the hotel.

A lot of people used to like cool drink in those days; nobody knew much about alcohol because we had no drinking rights yet. That was why there was empty cool drink bottles, and I used to get 'em refund. We take 'em back, bloke used to wash 'em and clean 'em and fill 'em with cool drink again. We used to take the bottles as we find them, whether it's clean or dirty, they clean 'em. Yeah, factory was like a big shed, with sections where they wash the bottles and fill the cool drinks.

All kind of cool drink was made there, Coca Cola, Fanta, ginger beer, he made all that in the factory. Only three or four people worked there, I saw them. Like Kalumburu had a machine too, and we made cold drinks with different colours. They used that strong liquid mixed with sugar and water in ordinary buckets. Brother used to make the coke liquid. Raspberry drink we made too. In Kalumburu, the cool drink machine came from New Norcia.

In Wyndham, one bottle was about two shillings and six pence (25c). I collect them in big bags or cardboard box. Bloke used to count 'em and give us money. I got £2 and ten shilling that time. I collect bottles only for a week, same time I was looking for a job. I wanted to work on the wharf, but they said nothing available. I asked around 'til I found one.

Finally I got a job at Shell depot near the goods shed, where all the goods are kept straight out from the boats. I worked there cleaning the fuel drums and filling them. I was spraying air inside and outside, just put air in—*shhhhhhhh*—just like that, and the dirt come out the other end, pressure bring 'im out. Drum has two holes, a big one and small one, one at each end. Before filling, they also put some sort of coating in to stop the rust. Then take it to the machine, click it, and as fuel comes that much from the top, it stop itself, automatic stop.

I used to go there every morning, about 8 o'clock I start; then knock off about noon or 2 o'clock, or work 'til afternoon. It all depends on how I like it. Me an' a white bloke used to work there for a month and a half. We didn't have to work all day. I got paid about £25. That was good money, not sure now if it was for a fort-night or a week.

The man who ran the cool drink factory was white. No Aboriginal people own anything in those days. He had white people work for him. Aboriginal people only brought the bottles. I didn't see white people do that. Aboriginal people were employed at Main Roads, on the wharf, public works. They work for big money in those days.

I used to live at Three Mile in single boys' quarter as you go in there, behind the Welfare Office. Accommodation was free. We only paid for food, I don't remember paying for accommodation. I used to sleep outside, can't sleep in there, too hot. We didn't have air-conditioning then. We didn't know about air-con, we never seen one, only the fan, you know.

We could get food, hunting in the hills. There are lots of kangaroos, old people had gun. I used to ask 'em to borrow the gun. The old people used to spear 'em too, still heap of kangaroos there now.

Soon it was nearly Christmas time, so I wanted to go back to Kalumburu. In Wyndham, I bought clothes, riding trousers, boots, clothes I had never seen before. I bought it in that Chinese shop there. The opposite one was Davidson Store, the white man shop. It had all the city clothes. White people had civilised clothes and things like that, city clothes. We knew Chinese people more than the white people. They were all right. Their shop had everything. A lot of people used to deal with the Chinese shop. Chinese people are good too. Chinese had mostly bushmen clothes. We were not fussy who is who.

I used to go to pictures here and there. We go with the taxi. Picture was in the meat works, a long way out, no bus. There was movie only one place, in the meat works. Movie theatre had two doors, one you went one side and you paid maybe two shillings, but the other side was for Aboriginal people. It was free. Seating was different. Long wooden seats were for Aboriginals and proper good seats for kartiya. If I wanted to sit in a good seat I would pay, but I didn't want to.

Inside we could see from everywhere. Heaps of Aboriginal people were there. One time at a meeting, Community Welfare complained that because Aboriginal people had to come with taxi from long way, they shouldn't pay for the movie. That's why it's free—don't know how true it is. There was also a kiosk there where people would spend money. Monday, Wednesday and Saturday they had movies, cowboy movies, black and white and sometime colour, Metro Golden Meyer (MGM). They had a big screen and a proper projector. Sometime proper live show used to come there, people like Slim Dusty and Buddy Williams.

Other times, we went walkabout to the shop. Sometime I just sit down there talking outside. Some people come from Forrest River Mission and camped there and we used to have a yarn with them. We walked everywhere. Once I walk all the way to the

Ambrose and his sister, Magdalene—Kalumburu Mission, 1950s

Ambrose approaching rock art site, Kalumburu 1996

In a rock art site, north of Kalumburu

At the grotto near Wyndham, 2001

Left: Ambrose's cousin brother, Micky Ngulben, c1953 (How Micky cheated the crocodile)
Right: Eugene Nanjimarra, Ambrose's father's brother (Old man Yogin)

movie. These days, people are spoilt. We used to walk to town. Walking is good, you can go here and there, in the car, you can't.

Because I worked some of the time, I still had some of that money from the mission when I went back to Kalumburu. Just before I went back, I asked Father Carl for it, half of it came back to Kalumburu with me. By then it was money time, too, in Kalumburu. People had some money for the first time; they were paid a little bit by the mission, then. Before they were not paid anything for their work. Some of the work was hard there and people did a lot of work.

No other boys or girls from mission got to go out to holiday. I don't remember any one else. I'm the only one because some of my family was there. My oldest brother, Brian, used to go up and down then and people that used to work at Forrest River before they went to town to work. They are dead now, you wouldn't know them.

After I came back to Kalumburu, Father Sanz asked me what I did in Wyndham. I told him and said one day I go out there and get a job. It was the first time I handled money in Wyndham. People told me what it was and I seen the others handle it. I couldn't check the change when I got any. You think they are honest because they are white people. I believed it then, I didn't realise they could cheat you. We never thought any of these thoughts before. I wouldn't have known if they cheated me.

You feed yourself in those days—that's what the police come around to check for on the Reserve in Wyndham. Aboriginal people there had to live with the jobs and the money. Vagrants get caught in town without a job. Like on patrol some time the police come look around. They go to the Reserve and ask Welfare first to get permission to go on the reserve in those days. Police come, drive around, pull up on the side and ask, talk to the people there, say, 'Hello, how are you?' Speak to the old people outside their houses. They ask people if they have a job. When they say, 'No', they ask 'Why not? Better find a job before next week or you go out to the station.'

Police used to go to the employer and ask how many and who is employed there to see if the people really work there. If not, they have to come to jail. If you have no job you go to jail for two or three months inside, that's how it was for vagrancy. That's pretty hard and tough. 'Righto, you have to go out and work somewhere,' police used to say. Sometime the station say, 'Full handed' or 'Come back 'til dry time'. Because then people are to still go somewhere, police say, 'It's a big country, go some other place, Broome, Halls Creek or Derby.' Sometime, Welfare sent 'em out when employer ring from station for workers. Welfare sent 'em out to work by plane then.

In towns, Aboriginal people had to live on reserves and they had to have work then. The meat works was there, too, operated in the dry season, closed in the Wet. There they employ many people and big crocodiles hang around where the blood was pumped into the sea from the slaughter yard. They killed 500-700 bullocks a day. Many carcasses. They came from the stations all around the Kimberley. The skin was put to one side, well packed and neat in good order.

Wyndham had a prison there too. Mostly Aboriginal people were locked up there, men and women, very few kartiya. They also had a government school and in the 1960s, they built a Catholic school. Wyndham had many people living there and the place was good for work and earning money.

Drink days

That's the time I walk out, when people I know came into the pub. You know why? They come and ask you to shout 'em drink and ask for money. I don't mind doing that, shouting drinks, but the other people only want you to buy all the time. That way you go broke quick; when I see no turns, I walk out with half the money still in my pocket.

I didn't drink for long time. I seen the others drink and get into violence, so I thought I try to see what I can do with it, to see what happened if I tried. In Kununurra, I tried to drink first time when I worked for Agricultural Department back in 1979, in September. I lived in the state house then in the town, not the reserve. I lived together with a lot of people. That old fellow, Alan Griffith and his wife Peggy, lived in this house somewhere near Lily Creek. They are friends, Mirriwung people. He's a funny fellow too, old Griffo.

I drank beer and I used to drink at home. I like the taste a bit at first, drank only one or two. I had tasted it before once, just a bit. I wasn't too sure about the taste then. I thought beer was good for the thirst; knock all the dust out from your work. I find out beer that people drink can make you hate your own family, because other people drink too much and get silly in the head, then they cause violence and disturbance and trouble. I used to drink a carton but I was still all right. When I know I'm getting drunk, I went home. I can start in the hotel or the club, go home later and still walk straight. If you mix drink you get sick, but I didn't get much effect even after half a night, seven or eight cans, and I leave some for next day. Man must have somebody to help him drink. I get some Oombi (Oombulgurri) boys or other people, or sometimes I drink with women. Only when lot of people come, I used to walk out.

You drink, you finally change yourself, your mind changes. What you see between no alcohol and alcohol there is two different things. The world looks different when you drink. I felt a bit happy sometime with the drink. With hangover, you feel like your head is boiling. You look for something to get over it, so you drink one more, then tea and coffee, and then I feel normal again. I used to walk home drunk sometime or get a cab. Sometime you have too much you get sick, too much whisky or brandy. I didn't like that, only wine or beer.

Well, I only wanted to drink sometime, because it is enjoyable when you drink with other people. Also it's not like having dinner or lunch. Drinking beer in a bar, you enjoy yourself because you meet many people and they tell you lot of stories from the bush or many years ago, when they used to drove cattle before the road trains came in.

After all, I find out that drink all the time is no good. One day I give up for six months; then I feel good myself. Some people used to have to go to the Dry Out Centre, but I have a strong power to control my own body and mind. I never went there. I give up for many years after that. I don't stay in the bar 'til I get blind drunk, only long enough to talk to friends. There were times when I used to drink worse than the others, because I drink two or three cartons in two days with one or two friends, but not in a pub, in a private house. I see others drink plenty, so I intend to drink much more than that. We also used to drink down by the river in Kununurra, near the Ord River Dam. We sit there for the day, take a fishing line, get a few bream and barramundi, have a fire and cook the fish. I have a friend called Mark Adrian. He was a taxi driver and he used to take me and pick me up again at night.

Now I only drink a little bit, a bit of wine and a few beers once in a while, and I enjoy that. I don't like getting drunk, it make bad publicity for the community. Aboriginal people get bad name.

This is a one man car

The first car I bought was $800. I had the money because I was working with the Agriculture Department. It was about 1979 when I started with them. Bit by bit I saved to buy that car. It was a Holden station wagon, light green. I bought it in Kununurra from Johnny Castledeane. He was a plumber, he knew me well and asked if I wanted to buy it. Seemed to be in good order, it didn't go for long trips. His wife only used it around the shopping area.

But I had a lot of trouble with it, break down all the time, going to Wyndham and back again. It was in the garage all the time. Still, I was satisfied. I love it, first time I own a vehicle like that which was my own private property. Some time we had to push it to make it start. After, when it was fixed again, it ran for long time—one month—and then something else went wrong with it. I didn't care how much I spent all the time, as long as I could drive it and it take me anywhere. That's all I thought at that time, never thought of complaining about breaking down, that wasn't in my mind yet.

Oh, I kept the car over two years. It used to break down all the time on long distance to Wyndham. In Kununurra it was all right. The radiator give way, it had a leak and I solder it myself. Petrol line it was all right. Later on, it give me too much trouble. I thought it might break down altogether, better off selling it to someone else. I wanted to buy 'nother one. Bloke want it from station, asked me if he could have it. He wanted to buy it and I said, 'I sell it to you cheap, if you give me $500 you can have it.' I told him few things wrong with it but he said, 'Nah, I work in a garage and fix it myself, I'll fix 'im up.' The bloke went to Doondoon Station. I didn't see the car again.

From there, I worked long time and then I got 'nother one, a Holden that was pretty good, more better. It was a Holden sedan, one that got boot behind it and was a brown, chocolate colour, about 1970 model. Bloke in tavern, he knew me. He worked for Public Works Department. He said, 'I never see you for long time.' Then he came and asked me, 'I never eat for one week, I have no food, I have a car there.' He had a few drinks there with a friend. He said 'I sell the car for $500'. I said, 'Yeah.'

I didn't look at the car. Well I had the money right there. It was tax return money and I had it in my pocket. I went and gave it to him. I counted—counted—counted, and said, 'Here's the money.'

The car was at the hotel. We walked down there, start 'em up all right. I didn't look under the bonnet or in the boot—I need it, it's all right. I took him there to the Ord River Dam where he camped and left him there. He gave me the papers. It was licensed. The car had a few holes in it on the side, but it was all right, still good.

I went to Wyndham in it and once hit a big kangaroo late at night. I couldn't stop, I tried to brake, but it was too close, so I had to hit 'im. It was still alive, so I had to hit 'im with a stone in the head. Then I lift 'im up and put it in the boot and load it up. Late, about eleven o'clock, I reached the old pensioners camp on my way to Wyndham. I turned off where the old people were drinking. I stopped and said, 'You want a kangaroo?' They all said, 'Oh yes!' Everyone jumped up and rushed to see. It was big enough to feed the whole camp and the dogs with it too.

So I drove up and down to Wyndham a few times and the car went well. The bloke had told me the oil leaks sometime, which it did. One night when I came back, the piston break, bearings in it had no oil in it. The engine went dry and cracked and hit the thing on the side. I stopped and looked with the torch. I nearly cried when I saw what happened. The oil gauge was out of order and I used to check it, but one day, I was a bit too drunk and forget. I was stranded. That was when these Aboriginal people came by and towed me in. I had two cartons, and one in the esky too. So they went to get a rope and came back and helped and we went to the camp in Leichhardt Street and had a few drinks.

Next day, they towed me to the garage and the people there said, 'What do you want to do with it, sell the spare parts?' I said, 'No, take this out and put new motor in.' They said, 'Yeah, we'll do that, will cost you $1,300 to bring it from Perth.' I was going to pay him, but he said, 'No, pay me when it's finished.' So they took it out and put brand new reconditioned motor in. Later on, it came on the truck, only took one or two days. I used to go to Halls Creek in that.

I had that car for a long time, three, four years, and it was good 'til I sold it. I left it with my friends Marko and Linda and told them I wanted to sell it but a bloke from a station want to buy it so I told him, I'll sell this for $800. I wanted to buy a new car. He gave me $800 cash, and Marko told me that I should have sold it for more money.

After that, I didn't buy 'nother car for long time. I didn't miss a car, I wasn't in a hurry, I didn't bother, I was on foot all the time. I didn't need a car. Later on I thought I buy another one. When I went to Perth I got one through the finance. I was thinking what car could I buy, that's all. In Perth, I made arrangements. I went to the car yard in Beaufort Street, somewhere there past the Beaufort Hotel and asked whether I could buy a car in this yard. One bloke sit in the office and when he see me, he come out to talk. He said this one has every bit of a new motor in it, 'I'm working on it, it been in an accident, it's nearly finished and ready to go out.' A Ford Falcon it was, automatic, 1983 or '84 model. I tried it out; I drive around in the city. Fella come with me. I did drive before in the city, someone else's vehicle, I been handling automatic before. He said, 'What do you think of it?' I said, 'all right, I'll have it.' He said, 'We'll arrange finance for you.' I told him I had a job and I arrange it from the bank, so I talked from Perth to Kununurra. The bank manager said, 'Yeah, his salary come in all the time.' He gave me good reference.

I did understand every bit of the finance sheet. I seen things like that before. Interest rate was 29 per cent. They did explain it to me and I knew how interest made things expensive. I didn't worry about any payments because it goes from the bank and I didn't have to worry about it. Money been paid from the office to the car yard. I earned about $800 a fortnight. In Halls Creek, I earned $1,000 a fortnight, because that was a long way in the bush. I had to pay $396 monthly. I gave them an extra hundred dollars to truck the car to Kununurra. I didn't want to drive it, I didn't know the way much.

Back in Kununurra, I wait and wait. Later on when I start work then, two or three weeks time, the car came. I got a call in the office. They put it up at Avis Rent-A-Car yard. When I went there, I got a docket and it said 'cash paid on collection'. I said, 'I'll be back tomorrow.' I went to the bank and then gave them $700 cash.

When I tried to drive the car, the battery was flat. It could not be charged and I bought a new one. I didn't care as long as the car was there. Then I couldn't drive it because it had run out of regis-tration. I went to the police station. They took it over the pit and Elgee Motor checked it out. 'Some time this afternoon, it will be ready,' they said. I told the Sergeant the car was all renewed in Perth. The car was clean, it had no rust, seat was pretty good, it had a radio, but that was out of order. I told them to put 'nother Alpine cassette player in, new speakers at the back, both sides. It was blasting out the back, the music. The car had a big aerial and I bought a roof rack. I was going to put a spotlight in too, but I didn't in the end. I bought the roof rack from Olivers' for twelve dollars. When I was away working out of town for the Agricultural Department, I left the car in the government car yard. It was locked at night and secure.

It was a good car. I used to go flat out in it and I didn't lend the car to anyone. I was a bit hard, I used to say, 'It cost me money to bring this car from Perth and I am in charge of it. I can drive you wherever you want to go, but I won't lend it. This is a one man car.' I lived there a long time with that car and then I went to work in Derby in 1992, and took the car with me.

There was only casual work in Derby. After six months, I couldn't get another job. There was nothing. Only the permanent people work there. I didn't have much money to pay for the car then, you know. I wanted to work in Derby for one year. From there I cannot afford to pay any more because I didn't have no job and the interest was too high. I had paid for that car for years and years. I still paid it off when I was already on Social Security, twice, but then it was bit too much money for me and I had to stop paying. The car also burned up a wire, I just couldn't start it any more, but it cost too much to fix.

In Port Hedland, I went to Legal Aid office next to the post office and asked them 'What can I do because I can't afford to pay any more for that car?' They said, 'You better off if you say you got bankrupt.' That's what they said to me. I come to Hedland on a bus because I want to study about horticulture at Pundulmurra College. I told them myself I couldn't pay any more, I ring 'em up, the finance, they said all right. I told them 'If you want to get it, it's at the Branco garage in Wyndham.' They took it when I was back in Derby.

At that time I didn't realise that I pay already $13,000 for the vehicle. That's very big money. I had little idea about that. If I had known I could feel sad to lose it, but I didn't know much about it. The price of the car was about $10,790 in the car yard, when I buy it in the early '80s. It was only later on I find out by showing the document about the finance statement to friends. Before I didn't talk to other people about this business. I keep it to myself, it had nothing to do with anybody. When people ask me I just told them I bought the car. The statement said that I had to pay $18,000 altogether for the vehicle, with interest and everything else. Esanda Finance Corporation was the finance company. When the car arrived in Kununurra, it had a flat battery, radio didn't work and no registration papers. I bought it in the early 1980s. I had it for a long time. When I gave the car back, I already pay $13,000.

After that, I lost interest. If I want anything now I pay in cash.

Chemical spraying for APB

When I live in Kununurra, I got driver licence. Before that I drove cars and station truck before I had a licence. In those days, it was good, the station people, the Aboriginal stockmen taught me how to drive. The manager let us drive the truck. I got it to the police station in Kununurra to get the licence. Had to fill out papers, passed them all, took me in a big truck for driving test, the big Mirriwung truck, drive forward without rolling back. I did it all.

Later when I worked in Kununurra with APB, the money was good. Then I didn't really worry about money. Now people are not satisfied. In those days when I hear other people compare with me, I was satisfied with what I was getting at APB. Only now I realise I was getting poorly paid and I was exposed to all those chemicals.

They paid about $400 or $500 a fortnight when I started with APB. Later I used to get about $800 a fortnight after tax. I save the money and own cars in those days. I was spraying weeds in Kununurra, parkinsonia trees, noogoora burr. The stations didn't like the weed. It goes on the stock and grows along the river. It prevents stock from getting to the river or being injured by the thorns. It's been found in East Kimberley, come from Africa. It grows along the water too. It grows too thick, and went on to the sheep stations, and cattle get the burr in the skin or the tail and then they spread it too. It sticks anywhere. Then there is the mesquite tree. It has thorns long as my finger. The first chemical we were using was 245 T, that's Agent Orange. They were using it in Vietnam, too, and we sprayed parkinsonia trees with it. I heard it was left over from the war in Vietnam and someone sell it to Australia. For a long time we didn't wear any protective clothing, just the clothes we normally wore.

I was using that spray near Lake Argyle, around Lissadell Station at the old homestead. I used to stay out, work for ten days in the bush. Start at six, knock off at three and get paid and then take four days off. For five months, we worked in the quarantine area along the Ord River 'til nearly holiday time. The rest of the year, we worked all over the place. Then we take airfare to Perth, or others drove off somewhere. We had free airfare and I stayed with friends, Martha and Rick, in Perth. They are from California and worked with me with the APB. They travelled around Australia and then bought a house in Perth.

Holiday lasted 'til after Christmas, from end of November. Six weeks we had off. We had holiday pay, too. I stayed in Perth for a few weeks, come back, go to Kalumburu and went back on the mail plane to Kununurra. I worked for APB for fourteen years.

We slept in swags at work and take our own food for ten days, do our own cooking. The APB supplied an Engel fridge with a little generator. We took tin meat, corned beef, a bit of everything. We load all the things in Kununurra on the APB truck.

We used to get very sick from spraying chemicals. Nobody realised, no one told us how dangerous it was. Nobody ever say much. Spray was mixed in a 44-gallon drum. Chemical was measured in a glass. It was a thick liquid. We mixed the chemical with diesel in the drum, three cups full of chemical in a 44-gallon drum of diesel. We shut the lid and then we put a tap on the drum, we drop it down and pour it out into spraying containers. The weed killer gets mixed around by the movement of the truck when we drove to the place where we spray. The drums were on the tray and we drive slowly, and then spray it all around on the weed in the bush. We also had six-gallon plastic spray packs. We used to carry it in the hand or we could carry it on the back. I like to hold it in the hand mostly and spray from there with the air pump. I didn't like to carry it on my back. Once it leaked.

They never warned us properly about the chemicals, they never explained to us properly. They said we must be careful not to let it go over us or spray against the wind. They should have said it could infect somebody. We didn't have protective clothing for it. We never thought of it getting into our bodies, we didn't know that could happen. When one of the boys, Dickie Gerard, died from the spraying, then straight away people knew nothing else killed him, because he was pretty healthy. After spraying, the skin in his face was changed, just full of sores everywhere, mainly in the face, nowhere else. Exactly he died over that, from the chemical that went in his face and he must have bin breathing it in. Somebody took a picture of his face. They must be hiding it now. Everybody knows it's from the chemicals he sprayed for about ten days, only that made him sick. He went to hospital and later he died there. You know Vernon Gerard, that's his family. They were brothers. I was still working then and I had sprayed for some time.

One time I was using a container on my back. The containers were second hand bought from the fire brigade. I was using one of them, and it sprung a leak. The chemical went everywhere. I didn't know it had a leak. We had no overalls, just ordinary clothes, a shirt and trousers what we buy from the shop. The chemicals went through the shirt all on my back. I took it off and wash myself in the river and then wash the clothes in the river. We always carried soap with us to wash our hands before we eat. I washed the chemicals off with the soap but I had to get the soap from the vehicle first. The chemicals went on my side, not so much on the back. From there I carried on work with 'nother container.

I was worried then. Dickie Gerard wasn't working with us yet. He was young and with a group learning how to do mapping. They were in the same area as we were spraying. We need one more man in our gang that time and that's how Dickie Gerard came to join us. Dickie worked for ten days with us and, after that, he developed that rash on his face. He was taken to Darwin hospital, where he died later from the chemicals. Some boys did tell him to be careful, but we didn't really understand ourselves about the dangers.

Sometime the wind blow the spray on to me, and the smell was very bad and made me dizzy. Several times when I went back to Kununurra, I got sick and wouldn't eat for a day when I came back from the spraying in the bush. We never thought it might do some other things inside our bodies. One old woman washed my work clothes. I told her not to touch it, I said, 'I wash that one', but when I went walkabout, she was washing it. Later on, she had skin rashes and they couldn't make out what it was. About a week later and little by little, her skin rash started getting worse. She went to Perth with that rash and later on, she died of the rash. In 1980s, they gave us protective clothes. For three years we had none. Only because somebody kicked up a stink about it after Dickie died, and straightaway we got a mask. People complained—Aboriginal people, the family of Gerard started to complain because their family member died. They were frightened in the APB office then, so in 1984, they gave us overalls, boots, gloves and mask. I used to wear my own hat. Sometime we couldn't use the gear because it was too hot to wear. It was only good for winter. They weren't made for this hot country. Because the money was good, I stayed in that job. It was good to work in the bush moving around all the time.

Two years before now the ALS (Aboriginal Legal Service) start an investigation into that chemical spraying and the sickness we got from it. Most of the people that worked with the chemical were Aboriginal. They couldn't find a doctor in WA that wanted to do that, so they got a doctor from Canberra. Well, he came and we had to fill out lots of forms. I travelled to Derby from Hedland on a bus to see that doctor for appointment. He examined people that work with that poison. I thought we might get compensation because we are all sick from it now. But doctor says he can't finish the examination because the WA government does not give the ALS more funding for the work. That's how that doctor can't finish. We get nothing and the people have died from it and nobody seems to care*.

---

* *Occupational Health and Safety are soon to carry out an independent inquiry into the chemical spraying in the Kimberley Region in the seventies and eighties.*

36/55

GOVERNMENT OF WESTERN AUSTRALIA

109

CLERK OF COURTS
WYNDHAM PORT 6741.

2nd September, 1969.

To
The Commissioner,
Native Welfare Department,
638 Wellington Street,
PERTH...W.A...6000.

Our Ref.......................

Your Ref.......................

Re: Application for Certificate of Citizenship
Brian SMITH.

Enclosed please find an application for Certificate of Citizenship and photograph applied for by Brian Smith of Wyndham.

Would you please return the appropriate papers at your convenience.

For your information Brian Smith was refused his application for Certificate of Citizenship on the 11th August, 1969.

R.J. Bremner.
CLERK OF COURTS.

In his own country... (see page 186)

contemporary
times

Oomarri trip

In August 1998, we left Port Hedland heading up to the Kimberley, up to my own country, Oomarri. We were going to spend some months there out in the middle of nowhere. I thought only the mining company Striker Resources is there. They explore for diamonds. Just before we set out we heard of several more mining companies also exploring in the same place. I was surprised to hear that. The Kimberley Land Council is supposed to inform traditional owners of such developments. The KLC has lawyers who are meant to keep track of what's happening on our land that's under Native Title claim. But do they do that? One mining company man told us that his company wrote to them but he got no answer, so that mining company just do what they like.

I went to Oomarri for a very good reason as I was appointed Warden for that country in 1997. I didn't get money for that job. We use our own money and our own resources to do that work. One tourist reported they found two skeletons up there at the sunset side of the waterfall, it was one big one and one little one covered in paper bark. I really don't know if it is an old burial side, that's why I thought to look. I have a fair idea of where to search. First I thought it might be the old man Yogin, who disappeared there. When they mentioned a little skeleton, I think straight away it wasn't the old man. He wandered away by himself, so I need to go up there and look. I am the one responsible for it. The skeletons belong to my people, may be my own family, because it's in the Oomarri area. I like to put a sign up there so no one would destroy the site. If one tourist found it, others might find it. I don't like people disturbing a burial place. Tourist did report it to the police in Kununurra and they informed Aboriginal Affairs in Perth. I heard it from a friend.

The police went there to look, but couldn't find access to the waterfalls. They drove with a vehicle one whole day in the area and couldn't find a way. My brother was with them but I believe he may not have wanted police to find the place. My brother has passed away now and I can't ask him.

The King George River flows into the Timor Sea. In the Wet the twin waterfalls come down in torrents from very high cliffs. It's very rugged country, and the river ends up shaped like a Y.

From Hedland, we went to Derby in our old four wheel drive and then on the Gibb River Road, pass through Kimberley Downs Station, past the Inglis Gap and Mt Barnett roadhouse and we camp at Gibb River Crossing. Once I saw an emu mother there with a chick. In the morning we went to Drysdale Station roadhouse, got fuel there, travel past Theda Station and on to Carson Station, where we stayed the night.

Carson River Station used to be run by Kalumburu, but last year people just walked off. Now it's deserted. Only the cattle are left. The house was ransacked and the horses are walking around in it. We made a bed inside but it was hard to sleep because there were a lot of bats flying around all night right above our heads, and they had a strong smell, too.

Next morning we took some paw paw from the trees, which were nearly dead for lack of water, and drove east to Drysdale River. We cross over, the water still running but not deep. We only come a short way up the other side when there was a loud noise like a shot and the engine stopped. Just where that happened, we were surrounded by small fires still burning from the night before. Big fire been through the place, we saw the glow in the dark from Carson Station. Kimberley is always like that in the dry season, lots of fires.

I tried my best to get the vehicle going, but we couldn't. We saw new fires burning in front of us and we couldn't stay there any longer. We bin there for hours. In the end we decided to walk back to the river crossing. We couldn't stay on the track because everything was burned black and dry, so we carried some of our things from the vehicle, lamp, one swag, some cans of baked beans and the gun and we walked back.

It was hot and we were tired from working in the sun. We worried about the car bin broken down and we didn't have no radio, only that EPIRB (Electronic Positioning Indicator Radio Beacon) to use. By then, it was lunchtime and we thought we better let it off. On that track nobody goes up and down much, I could be sitting there for weeks and months with no help, so we let it go. We were held up in Hedland before we came and were already late, and not a lot of time was left 'til the rain comes again. Some years the Wet comes early. EPIRB is a little thing like a radio; it's set up in such a way it sends a signal to the satellite. It's an electronic signal; the satellite picks it up and passes the message to the emergency station. By late afternoon they found us, a fixed wing spotter plane came and circled. Later on it was a chopper making a huge noise. It came round and round looking for a place to land. That isn't easy because the area is very rugged.

Finally we got on and we went up. I never bin in a helicopter. We were glad we got away from the fires. They took us to Troughton Island. There are oilrigs in the Timor Sea and a maintenance crew lives on that island. I did recognise the place because I worked there once before a long time ago. So we stayed there. It was like a five star hotel. What wonderful food we ate there! The people were very nice to us and we thanked them for the rescue. They said, 'We enjoyed that, it had a good ending.' We could watch a whale and her baby play around close by in the water. We enjoyed living there for two nights, but worried about the car. On Tuesday morning the island managers kindly arranged a flight from the island to Kalumburu. As we landed, two girls were sitting on the runway with a dog, watching the sunrise, and the pilot was worried about coming down near them, but we made it.

We got picked up by a new clinic Sister and straight away look for someone to drive us out to our vehicle and a mechanic to fix the car. I found one of my relations, asked for help and they said, 'Yeah, we'll take you.' My relation had a friend, a mechanic staying there, and he came too, along with other boys. They drove a long way out to Drysdale River, passed Carson River, and we found the car still in one piece. The mechanic was able to fix the car in a short time. The timing had come out on the rough Gibb River Road. My cousin shot a bush turkey and a killer, gave us some meat for the road, and went back to Kalumburu. They were happy they got some good meat.

From there, the car was going good and we went straight to the place we wanted to go. The road was pretty rough and there were many more fires burning. But we made it to the mining camp without trouble. The people who rescued us, been asking the mining camp before if they could help with the car and they said they would tow it to Kalumburu for us, if we couldn't get it fixed. Now I told the camp manager we were all right and they didn't have to do that. We stay in the mining camp for one night.

The manager told us we couldn't use the track going near the waterfalls because his men got bogged there badly. That was bad news. We had rung the camp before we went on the trip and checked on the roads and they told us they were all right. We been on that track before. It is the only one going near the falls. We intended to make camp there and then walk about four kilometres to the waterfalls.

We even organised petrol supply before we left. I had written a letter to the mining company to ask them if they could take a 44-gallon drum of petrol into the bush on one of their trucks when they take in their own fuel. There is no service station, nothing, in the area. If you don't have fuel to drive around there and out again, you can't go in; you'd have to walk out. The company said they take our fuel if they got room on the truck. I didn't like that much, I couldn't rely on them—what if we get there and there is no fuel for us? We got the feeling the company didn't like us to go there, what's one more drum on their big fuel truck? So we managed to get the fuel in with 'nother mining company called Dioro. A nice man called Luis said to my partner on the phone in July before we start on the trip, 'No trouble, I'll take that in for you tomorrow.'

I was very glad about that and we thanked him. If he hadn't helped us we could not have gone. The Striker Resources Company that explore in my country for long time now, did not take in any fuel for us even though I asked them. That was disappointing because I am the traditional owner. They explore on my land for diamonds that really should belong to me and when once I ask them to do something for me, they don't do it. Such a small thing! They have made an agreement with my people and the Kimberley Land Council. I have never seen it but ask for it many times.

My partner asked the camp manager if they could give us an escort in on the boggy road, and at first he said yes. Next day he changed his mind. He might've been talking to the office in Perth, I don't know, perhaps he was told what to do. He himself is a good man. He was very helpful later. At the time he said we could go to a tourist camp on the coast about fifty kilometres from the mining camp. He said that because the man who runs it has a boat, he thought we might get to the waterfall that way.

Now I need to talk a bit about that tourist camp. It's not far from the waterfall and is still my country all along there. I know the man who built that place up, a white man; he used to be a donkey shooter. We decided to see him because that seemed to be the only way I could get to the waterfall.

That man make business with the tourists there, he take 'em fishing, and has accommodation for them. He went there without consulting Aboriginal people. He didn't come and ask me. It is my own country and he didn't ask me or people in Oombulgurri. He set the business up quietly. When he finished everything we found out, a taxi driver told me. Later on he invited us to go and see that place, but we didn't have time then. So I thought now I can go and ask him to take us to the waterfall. Same time I might talk to him about a deal if he wants to stay there. I wanted to get rid of him for a long time now; I don't want him on my country. He didn't consult any of us. I wrote to the KLC several times and over several years, and didn't get response still today.

The track into that camp is like a creek bed at first. We had to get out and move the big river stones so we could drive over them safely, only very slow. On the side of the track we found some rock painting and we looked at them. Then, as we came to the jump-up, it was very hard going, we had a heavy load on and the track was totally washed out. Later we passed a beautiful billabong with water lilies. Finally we came to where the house was. We had to drive down a very steep track on a mountain.

Well, the owner was away. 'Nother man was in the camp, an offsider, who work for him, don't know his 'nother name. He offer us a cup of tea and said owner will be back in a few days. Then, when he heard we wanted to stay there and wait for him, he didn't want us there; he didn't want me there, especially. He said he had his guests come in the aeroplane. We told him we had our own supply. We wasn't going to stay in his house, I just wanted to find a place in that camp, so we didn't have to go back in the bush and go in and out waiting for the owner. Still he said the place was "exclusive" and people may not like to see traditional owner there. When we told him his boss invited us, he was more friendly but still wanted us to leave.

Because he said he'd talk to the boss on the phone that evening, we asked him to see if he (his boss) could bring back a pair of springs for us when he gets back soon. Our back springs had gone flat with the load and we were worried about them breaking. We said we'd pay for them. The man said he'd ask the owner, but he still pushed me out of my own country and asked us to camp in the bush. I didn't want to stay then and left.

Next day he came out to our camp and was rude and arrogant, told me that to get springs, it cost me over a thousand dollars for the parts and the air charter, and $800 to take us to the waterfall and the return time could not be guaranteed, that depend on his guests, when they want to go to the waterfall. The following day he told us that he'd called the Striker Resources office in Perth and that he was told there were springs for us already in the mining camp near us, and that we should go there. He also urged me to drive along 'nother track which he said would get us to the waterfall. I did try the track and it ended up nowhere. Later 'nother fella told me in the mining camp that he almost got lost on that same track.

That fella said a lot of things to get rid of us, make us leave that place. He told me lies. He said they don't do things for nothing there. We offered to pay for the trip to the waterfall, but $800 is a big money. He also told me that it takes three and a half to four hours to get there in the boat. Later two Telecom fellas told us that they got taken for free to the waterfalls and it took only 40 to 50 minutes in the same boat. That happened just some days after that man told me they didn't do anything for nothing.

He didn't even know when he would pick us up again from the waterfall. We couldn't trust him to take us there, he might take us and never come back, place is so isolated that anything could happen to us. He didn't allow me to stay there or to make telephone call from the camp and from there we couldn't trust this man so we decided to leave. We did go to the mining camp and we told them that the man told us that they had springs for us. They said, 'No, we don't have any springs, we'd have to take them off our vehicles.' So we knew for sure how that fella told me a heap of lies just to get me out of my own country.

After that we look for 'nother camp, and we found a place called Python Pool. I really don't know what place that was, but when we found it, I saw it was my birth place. That is the place we call Oomarri, the place I was born, where I was given my totem *junggao*, the lizard. That's the place the old people told me about. They said Oomarri is where the big mountains are, permanent waterhole, big spring. The way the waterhole is shaped like a python's head, that's why the white people give it that name, but we don't call it that. I never forget for a long time that I was living there now. I was so happy that I found it again.

We stayed there and I hunt and fish, and explore the place. We did discover lots of paintings of my own ancestors that lived there, where they use to dance the junba. My tribe is the one that lived there before. We walked across the river on a big log, climbed up the mountain, see lots of painting, many very old, all done by my people before me. They are gone but I am here and the painting is still there, like big art galleries full of it, so beautiful! I also found lots of spearheads, some really big, others small and very sharp, made out of quartz and other stone, and several grinding stones.

Walking around, make me think a lot about my country and it was good that I did—been away so long. I was so happy to see that place again and I want to go back again soon. I could return, live off the land for a while, maybe build a house there. Is good at night there with the pleasure of the bush, you see sunrise and sunset, so enjoyable. We sleep under the stars, away from city lights. We hear dingo howl, and different owls call, flying foxes roost, and I hear my friend the kookaburra laugh. We ate a few ngarlaworri (bush apples) but the flying foxes eat most of them each night. It was good eating real bush tucker again, but hunting is not so easy when you get older. There are too many fires all the time and not as much left to eat now, even with a gun. Still there are wallabies, ducks and bush turkeys, lots of snakes, birds, frogs and yaourr (water goanna). I had to kill one king brown snake 'cause it had come under our bed. In the middle of the day when it's hot, we sleep in the shade. It's a good life.

We enjoyed our stay in the bush, in my country, and being there made me feel real good. But I couldn't look for the skeletons because I couldn't get near the place. We called Aboriginal Affairs from the mining camp to see if they could find some money for us to fly to the waterfall by floater plane from Kununurra later, seeing that I was already up there in the Kimberley, but they never even gave us a reply at all, though we asked them to. I tried to get another man in Kalumburu to take us in his boat, but it was under repair in Darwin, and there was some trouble about getting it back to Kalumburu. There was no one else to take us.

I am still worried about the skeletons and I want to try again to find them.

A warden's job

From Kalumburu to King George River there was nobody to take care of the country. No warden appointed to look after the area, the bush and Aboriginal sites. I wrote to Aboriginal Affairs Department in Perth and told 'em that I wanted to get that job. I wanted to be warden because that is my tribal country, my people lived there, and I know the area.

It's very hard to travel through some of that country, road is pretty rough, 'specially when the weather change and the rains come. When I apply to become warden I was living in Kalumburu recording Aboriginal history with my partner, Traudl. We lived there for about a year. Appointment didn't come 'til about nearly ten months later. I did everything that I could, but it take Aboriginal Affairs long time to make the appointment. I was in Kununurra at the time, and was asked to go to Aboriginal Affairs. They just gave me paper and took me picture there. Paper was a letter from the minister that I was appointed. They said there'll be training very soon, like next month, for a warden, so I can know what to do, how to do the job and what's what. I don't know what happened to that training. I had to wait for 'nother twelve months—no—'til end of December 1998, that I finally got some training when we were in Perth. I went to Aboriginal Affairs one day just to have a look to see if I could get a badge for being a warden, to show other people when I'm doing the job, and they tell me 'bout the training. I needed to go to the bush so I asked for a badge, some form of identification, but I didn't get any. I don't know, they just didn't bother enough—they said it wasn't ready. It means they didn't exactly care.

After I was appointed, it took almost two years and then finally, finally, when I came to the city—after I'd been on a big journey on the warden job—that they came up with the badge. It was so easy; they could've done it straight away.

Training took only from 9.30 am to noon on one day, that's all, two and a half-hours. Others was there too, people who were appointed from other communities, Bidyadanga and from south, about six wardens altogether or seven.

A white person did all the training. She was talking to us all, and people ask her what all this meant, the warden's rules. In this place, in the city, I notice Aboriginal people always ask questions, not like in the Kimberley. She said what responsibilities are and the rules, and about the Heritage Act, about any trouble if people might destroy anything in the bush or in sites, or if you ask the owner of a property to let you in, you show him the card and say I am entitled to go through, these things. I look through the Heritage Act several times, too, but it's written so people can't understand it easily.

I was telling 'em about how we went there to Oomarri in '98. I told 'em about the skeletons the tourist found two years ago and how I need to check it out. Might be it was a burial site. We went there with our own expense; we didn't get money from anybody. My own pension money, that doesn't take you very far. Lucky I had that money from the lotto. That one helped with the petrol. I won that money, about $1,100, all that I used on the trip too, for fuel, mostly. We didn't have brand new vehicle, we have '83 model Toyota Landcruiser, bit old now. My partner had bought that four wheel drive so we could travel in the bush. We were lucky to have that vehicle. At the same time we had a chance to make that special trip to go to my country. We bin up and down the Kimberley many times. For this big trip as a warden, vehicle had to have repair done, parts and spares we had to buy and two new tyres put on. When you live up north you can't save much, there's a high cost of living, petrol, gas and food are all much more than in the city.

We never made it to the skeletons, because when we got there, the road was inaccessible. We tried all sort of ways; we try to arrange it from the mining camp through the satellite phone, but it cost $1800—from Kununurra to the King George River waterfall and back. We ring Aboriginal Affairs from the mining camp right in the middle of the bush, and ask couldn't we get that money from somewhere, could they find out for us, please! They said, 'We are not a funding agency' and that first we had to apply for funding. We had already explained we were in bush in the middle of the Kimberley in a tiny mining camp, only about 30 or 40 km away from the waterfall where the skeletons are. We ask 'em to try their best, we gave 'em telephone and fax number and tell 'em we would be back in exactly a week's time, same time, same phone and could they please let us know then. Next week we drove 50 km over rough tracks to the phone again but nothing was there, no telephone call, no fax. Aboriginal Affairs didn't even bother let us know anything. We were disappointed to find nothing. Make me feel no good; I was upset about it. We thought because we come such a long way and got so close to reaching the place I needed to go, that they would try and help.

We come very long way with our own money. That trip bin very carefully planned. We didn't expect that problem. We bin in that area not long before and knew the track and the country, only the last bit we couldn't do. The last big Wet had sanded up the track. I was so close to it, to find the skeletons. We bin come such a long way. To drive there and back from Port Hedland is about 3,500 km.

While we lived in the bush, we found a fresh pile of rubbish in a very remote place at the King George River. We even took photographs. It was just alongside the riverbed. We knew the place; we had camped there before. At first, from a distance, I thought it was a camping gear. Then we saw it was pile of rubbish, heaps of empty beer cans, Victoria Bitter, three or four carton, lots of other empty food tins, meat trays, sausage wrapping, film wrappings, cigarette packets, egg carton and other rubbish, and it all came from Broome and Kununurra. You could still see the price tags.

We asked the Striker Resources manager later 'bout it, but he said his boys drink a different kind of beer, Emu Bitter, green cans. That's true; we saw their cans in the mining camp. But it was several mining companies there now in the area, so we don't know. Very few tourist go there, place is too remote, no shops, no fuel. People that left the rubbish never bothered burying it. I never seen rubbish there before—you won't see it any more now because flood water in the Wet take it away down stream over the waterfall, to the sea.

This is my country and it's very beautiful, clean sand, clean air, clean trees, everything is clean. People shouldn't leave nothing there; they have no right to spoil the country and dump their rubbish, that's a bad thing to do. They should take it back with 'em like they do it some other places I saw, like in Bungle Bungles. They don't care things they leave behind look ugly. It can hurt animals and spoil the bush. The bush grow up on its own. That rubbish is made in the factory, it don't belong in the bush, it looks bloody ugly there. I'd like to put a sign there next time, explain why rubbish shouldn't be left behind in bush.

Later on we saw 'nother thing at a place near Horrocks, just out from Northhampton on the coastal road going south. When we came back from the beach, I noticed an Aboriginal site with paintings and caves near the road. A sign bin put there by Aboriginal Affairs. It bin shot through with bullets, five or six shots. Look like target practice to me. I thought in my mind, Oh, hell, who could do that! Straight away I think it means that, before, not long ago, Aboriginal people were shot, and now they shoot our signs. Painting and caves there belong to Yamatji tribe. Don't know where all the Yamatji people live there, we couldn't see any in the town, not like in Roebourne or Derby up north, place is full of Aboriginal people.

Aboriginal Affairs know it is a sign there. At that training session for warden in Perth I told 'em it bin shot through. Aboriginal people there all said that's wrong; they all speak up down there. I said that sign should be replaced. Aboriginal Affairs said something like Yamatji people has to do that, or apply for that. That's why I thought we might look there again one day. Maybe Yamatji people not see that yet. What's wrong with me telling Aboriginal Affairs? I'm a warden too and I report it.

I think this warden business must be done more better. I applied to become a warden in 1996. Nearly a year later I was appointed, and training I didn't get 'til end of 1998. When I had bit of trouble and needed help, there wasn't any available. How can warden do their job properly and take care of our Aboriginal heritage sites when we have no good vehicles, no money for fuel to get around, and no help from Aboriginal Affairs, at all? The bush and sites must be looked after, not only for Aboriginal people. There are some other good people in this country who know how to appreciate Aboriginal heritage, too. The government only talk, but they don't do enough. They only get a move on quickly if they can see money coming.

I see old people dance again

About twelve months ago I mention our dances. That time I felt they must be dying out 'cause I didn't see many people continue with them, except old Basil Djanghara in Kalumburu. He did a very good job trying to keep some dances going, but he had some trouble and not much help. Now, this week in the city, I see the Gija dancers came along from the Kimberley and dance here. I was happy to see that and want to add that to my 'nother story 'bout dancing, to make it right.

Quite a few people among the dancers I knew very well, one from Turkey Creek, 'nother few from Gibb River, most from Yulumbu and Imintji. They brought that junba dance and the wungga dance. I haven't seen that for a long time. Last I seen junba was at the Boab Festival back at the end of 1980s in Derby. That was Mowanjum junba, from Derby area.

Each community does its own junba. It's owned by one person and his tribe, but other people can dance it too. Wungga is danced with the didjeridoo music, you can see it everywhere, like in Arnhem Land, and they can all dance it. Some call it lirrga, same thing. Junba is done by tribes people in a particular area, that's why communities like in Turkey Creek (Warmun) have got their own. Old Rover that passed away, he owned that junba, Rover Thomas, the artist painter. He made that balga song, and when he passed away people still dance it.

In the city lot of Aboriginal people enjoy the Gija dances. Maybe they never seen a dance like that before. Even the old people came with the dancers, some of them first time they ride on Ansett, never bin in the city. I told 'em last night, million people live here, I tell 'em whenever you drive out of the city here everything is fenced, you can't go anywhere now down here. In the Kimberley there are fences, too, but much of the country is still free. Fences might come later; I hope they don't. Along the Gibb River you can sleep anywhere you like, there are no fences all over the place like down here.

Gija is a language, and dancers are all mixed, little bit from that side tableland area, Yulumbu, Mount House side, they call it all flat country, Gibb River and Derby. They enjoy bringing the show too, they're here for two weeks, and from here they go south. Mostly all the dancers are old men, only one was young, the son of the man that was singing. They brought young boys with them, the teenagers. They train the young boys in the dance, that's what they said, they keep themselves going, they take 'em so the young ones keep away from grog—some young girls came too.

Dances was pretty good, junba dance specially. See, the sound of didjeridoo down here is different, they all got different ways, and the Kimberley one is different too. Jimmy Webb from Fitzroy and Richard Walley from Perth play didjerodoo different, they pronounce the sound different with their lips, like talking lips, that's how the sound comes out. All depends what people want to dance, the clapstick strike together to mark the rhythm itself. When they dance junba, they don't use the didjeridoo. With junba they tell you what it's all about. Stories like how they lost their way, sleep in the creek and are disturb by mosquitoes, or like the young man pinch the old man's wife. That girl talk on the microphone to make people understand what the culture of the Aboriginal people was from long time ago, and the old people sing.

Dancers they paint up and dress up, paint up proper just like when they go hunting. That's how they wear hair belt, too, did you see? That made of human hair, they make it themselves, just like in some painting you see on the rock, the *Guyon Guyon* painting. Yesterday the dancers paint bracelets around their arm, and dot lines on their face. They wear red loincloth; women had long red skirts for dance, that's how it looks good at night. In the wung-ga dance the group came out, sing all the way like that, 'til they come to the sitting place. Women and all come there to dance bit by bit, little by little. In the end they get up and sing and dance, 'til they finish.

This is traditional dance from the old people themselves, not new dances. They just want to share the dance like they did in the old days. I did understand some of the Gija language.

To perform the dance means a lot for Aboriginal culture, it keeps it alive and I feel very good about what I saw, yes. It was also good they brought young people with them to train and to show 'em what the city is like. One day, when they grow older, their turn to do the dances.

I was very pleased to see somebody still doing the dances today and take it to the city and all around. Same time I met all the old friends I know from mustering. That was very good and I enjoy it very much.